Voice in the American West

Andy Wilkinson, *Series Editor*

Also in the series

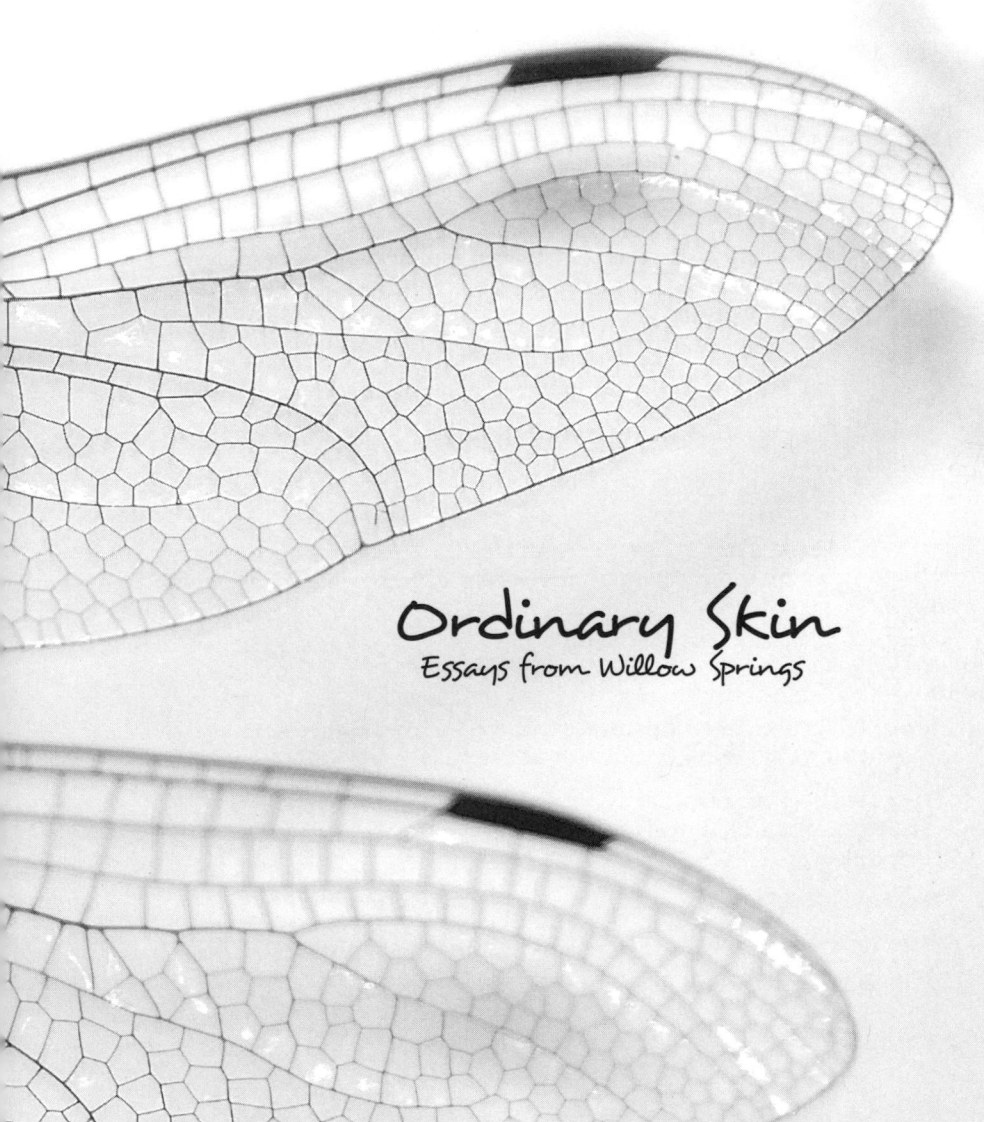

Ordinary Skin
Essays from Willow Springs

Amy Hale Auker

Texas Tech University Press

This book is typeset in Perrywood MT. The paper used in this book meets the minimum requirements of ANSI/NISO Z39.48-1992 (R1997). ∞

Designed by Kasey McBeath

Library of Congress Cataloging-in-Publication Data
[CIP TK]

17 18 19 20 21 22 23 24 25 / 9 8 7 6 5 4 3 2 1

Texas Tech University Press
Box 41037| Lubbock, Texas 79409-1037 USA
800.832.4042 | ttup@ttu.edu | www.ttupress.org

"Using Tools Backwards" first appeared in *Ranch & Reata*, issue 2.4, 2012, and again in *Ankle High & Knee Deep*, June 2014, ed. Gail Jenner.

"Ugly Mud Bugs" first appeared as "Mixed Metaphors" in *Cowboys & Indians*, January 2013, and with current title in *Ankle High & Knee Deep*, June 2014, ed. Gail Jenner.

"But Now I Ride" first appeared in *Cowboys & Indians*, January 2014.

An early version of "Infinite Pink" appeared online at Stevie Zine, May 2014.

"Willow Springs" appeared in *Range*, Fall 2015.

To Gene and Barbara Polk, who gave us the gift of this ranch

Barn's burnt down, now I can see the moon.
~Mizuta Masahide, seventeenth century samurai and poet

Contents

Contents

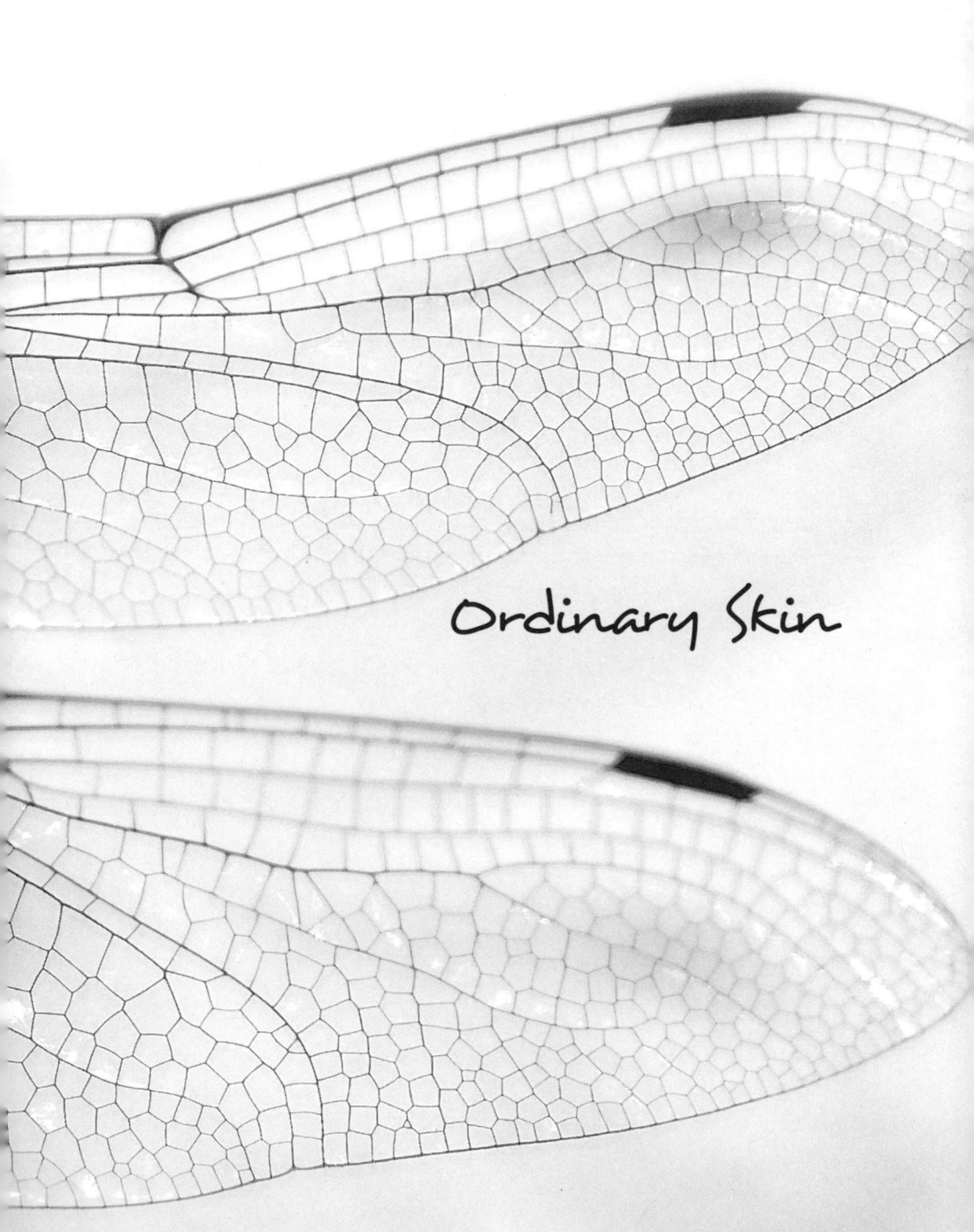

Ordinary Skin

Ordinary Skin

And then there is this waiting in my wings, almost as if they miss the flapping awkwardness of getting off the ground, the effort and struggle to leave the dirt and comfort of earth, but I am not sure they remember the soaring.

And then there is this feeling of fins and gills, as if I should rest on the bottom of the ocean for a measure, a beat, with its weight as my blanket and its roar as my song.

And then there are these phantom claws growing from my fingertips, aching to dig into the rich damp earth and burrow deeper, get soil in all my crevices so that I might taste from whence I came.

And then there are these words . . .

There is, in the back of my throat, the smell of my lover's skin and blended juices and night.

There are these shimmering scales and iridescent feathers and silky hairs that catch the light and throw it firmly back into the day.

And I snuggle down into my ordinary skin.

Glow Time

Our mornings often look like this: rise from the bed together, spread up the sheets and blankets, dress, and brush our teeth. He goes out to feed the horses, hollering "shut up, shut up, no barking" at the excited dogs. They think he is barking along with them. I put on coffee, fry bacon, scramble eggs, and toast English muffins. Books, pens, paper, topo maps, copies of the *New Yorker, Western Horseman, The Sun,* and *Good Old Boat* litter one end of the long table. The owner's manual for the compressor, "No Trespassing" signs, work gloves, tools, and earplugs for when we cut firewood are stacked on the other end. There is no television here, and our phones and computers live in other rooms. Mornings are for the big windows all around, the sills loaded with stone *manos* and flint knives, points and pottery, a few cobwebs, always cobwebs. I carry a coffee can of birdseed to the tray hanging from the oak tree outside and, in the spring and summer, spoon grape jelly into orange halves. I've made grape jelly junkies of the orioles, the tanagers, the grosbeaks, and even the house finches.

My arrival at Spider Ranch in the fall of 2008 was based on the idea that Gail Steiger and I would work cows together. Labor was to be the test of our newborn relationship. E-mails, phone calls, and cowboy poetry gatherings had been our courtship as we each endured the earthquakes of separation and divorce. We both had big holes in our chests as relationships around us broke and then reformed along new lines. It turned out that work was what made us strong, saved us, gave us firm footing for being in love. As Gail said during that first year, "You can't fall out of bed when you're lying on the floor."

I owned a fairly new handmade saddle, but I had never carried a rope or felt it tighten around a calf. There was no seed tray hanging outside the window of this home, and I had no idea that the *New Yorker* sometimes publishes a fiction edition. I have since become a short story junkie. The next spring when Gail helped me hang hummingbird feeders, it felt like an act of love. Now, a male Anna's stays all winter and I look forward to the arrival of the fierce Rufous in August.

This collection of essays and prose poems is less memoir and more a reflection of my settling-in process over several years, my discovery of a new landscape, though the word *landscape* seems weak. It cannot begin to touch this place, this dirt, this water. Spider Ranch is seventy-two square miles of varying terrain, from 6100 feet above sea level to 3400 feet, from Ponderosa pines and bears to catclaw and cactus wrens. The trails are either straight up or straight down and are connected by long mesas covered in non-stop volcanic rock.

My adjustment has been about labor and love and community, even about the dreaded empty nest as my children have grown from complicated teenagers into delightful, but just as complicated, young adults. It has been about learning to cook for only two people, my pottery bread bowl standing empty most of the year. It has been about a completely new bookshelf, a new playlist, a new way of moving through the world.

And in true love-story fashion, it is also about a man . . . a man who chose the life of a peasant, growing food on untillable land in spite of a university education and skills as a documentary filmmaker and singer/

songwriter. Like most of the cowboys in Texas, my father got a copy of *Ranch Album* for Christmas in 1987, so I was familiar with Gail's work and Gail's voice long before I actually met him at the Texas Cowboy Poetry Gathering in 2007. *I see a rider, over the hill. Maybe he doesn't know yet, time don't stand still.* I stepped outside to call my friend Ross Knox. He said, "Oh, keep your pants on. He's just another cowpuncher." That was long before I knew how blue Gail's eyes are or the tone that files his voice into a hard edge when he feels taken advantage of. Long before I knew that he doesn't know how to say no. Long before I knew how unbelievably strong he is; how he always lifts the heaviest end of everything. Long before I knew that he leaves pieces of himself behind on stage when he sings for an audience. Long before I knew what a slob he is, though he tried to tell me in a late-night e-mail, probably the same one in which he told me about the scorpion that ran up the inside of his sleeve and stung him five times. I asked him if he took some Benadryl and he said no . . . he medicated with Natural Ice, an efficient beer for the situation. That was before I knew that he kills scorpions that come indoors but carries centipedes outside in the dust pan, unharmed. That was long before I knew his sense of humor, dry asides that define the world and people around us and leave me gasping with laughter. Before I knew how much he likes junk food and sushi or that he has ridden the same saddle for thirty years and isn't sure he's gotten his money's worth, and that he listens to very loud music on long road trips. That was before I knew how lonely he was, how he didn't need me to cook or clean or do his laundry, tasks I had done for men all of my life. He needed me to get on my horse and ride. This is a big place, and he'd been working alone for too long. That was before I knew how much he loves this ranch, how much he loves cows, how much this piece of land has taught him and how much he wanted to pass some of that terrain- and place-specific knowledge along. Long before I knew that he was so much more than just another cowpuncher. *I see a cowboy over the hill. Maybe nobody told him, time don't stand still.*

I can think of no greater kick than being transplanted in the middle of life, no greater or more welcome challenge than being bent and softened by a steep learning curve in my fifth decade. Others who have made similar shifts have stories to tell, and mine includes a seven-week camping trip in 2006 as a trial separation from my first husband. I'd never been camping or hiking outside of Texas, never explored public lands. During the transition, I also worked for a pack station in the eastern Sierras for two seasons, served cocktails on the South Rim of the Grand Canyon, and then circled back around to living once more on a commercial cattle operation. The same, and yet, oh, so different. My transplanting, from Texas to California to Arizona, brought me to these mountains at just the right time.

To learn to love the Texas Panhandle, I had to embrace the wind. I had to make myself go outside and crunch the grass beneath my feet. I was desperate enough to seek out even the beauty of the broom weed. Here in the Santa Maria Mountains, all I have to do is lift my eyes to the rocks, especially during the evening glow time—that ten minutes of magic when the granite boulders turn pink-orange. All I have to do is stumble into the damp crease of a canyon, alive with dripping water and covered over with a carpet of moss. All I have to do is think of my encounters with the bat, the fox, and the Gila monster's half smile. The mariposa lily and the sego lily. The wasp galls on the oak leaves. The bees resting deep inside the cactus blossoms. The mud and the work.

Frog Sex

We all thought they were doing it—the frogs and toads of childhood, those tightly clasped pairs with seemingly fragile, and yet strangely strong arms that we tried to pry apart. That was back when we still played in the mud.

The summer I was nine years old was all about sex. My mother had just announced her fourth pregnancy. I had a crush on the hired hand, and the dark-skinned men in the bunkhouse fed my sister rattlesnake meat. By August, I had a urinary tract infection.

That was the year my father and his business partner leased eighty sections of ranchland in far West Texas just in time for an unprecedented summer. Most of the ranch got thirty inches of rainfall in an area that normally averaged eight. The pastures grew plants rarely seen in the region, like pretty dodder, a parasitic vine that twined around everything with strange yellow and orange tendrils. The old men, like my grandfather, exclaimed and told stories of other lush years. Every low place became an unaccustomed lake. And there were toads. We called them frogs, of course, and we thought they were doing it.

That was the summer my mother spent a long hot afternoon throwing rocks and sticks and my brother's Tonka trucks at the biggest rattlesnake anyone could remember to keep him from crawling under the house until my father could get home. She sent me running to the corrals when we heard the cattle coming in. It took me quite some time, standing on the silver pipe of the corral fence, to get my father's attention, to get him to see me. He was visibly irritated when he rode through the dust to yell, "What?" in my direction. I rode the half mile back to the house behind his saddle, my arm aching where he'd swung me aboard. When he reined up in the wagon yard, he flipped the keeper on his lariat rope aside so he could use the heavy hondo to kill the snake.

"What's that sound?"

The whole afternoon reverberated with the noise of many rattles. I still remember him putting his rope back on his saddle horn and going into the house for his gun.

That was the summer I rode my bike to the mailbox every third day for zippered pouches of Books-in-the-Mail, a library lending program for rural families. I spent hours circling selections in the included catalog, next week's reading material. In previous summers, my sister and I had loaded our little red wagon with books to be returned and walked down the dusty streets of Van Horn, across a vacant lot, a total of five blocks to the old school that housed the county library. The wood floors and dim, chill stacks were a startling relief to the bright sunlight glaring off caliche and asphalt. We blinked hard when we emerged with new books, new stories to be bumped home. We were allowed to stop at the playground but usually the slides and swings and monkey bars were burning hot in midday so we passed on by.

That was the summer I dreamed of being homeschooled instead of going back to live at our house in town ninety miles to the south. I read every word in the Calvert Course brochures until my mother told us she had decided to have the new baby in town rather than so far from a hospital.

That was the summer my father hired a kid from New Zealand to break colts, and more than anything, I wanted to sit on that dark-headed young man's lap. That was the summer my sister and I memorized poems from the *Little Golden Book of Poetry* and recited them while standing on the stone hearth at one end of the living room. The hired hand's bed was in the other end. The poems were childish, but I remember the feeling of Robert Lewis Stevenson as he filled my mouth with the idea of shadow. That was the summer I slept in a twin bed tucked into a corner. My mother must have furnished the ranch house by going to garage sales because my dresser was a piece of nursery furniture, a clothes closet cabinet flanked by drawers with alphabet building block pulls. I loved it.

That was the summer moths, called Miller bugs, infested everything and left dirty yellow smears on windows, surfaces, and bedding.

My father's business partner lived in the ranch house, too. He did not have children, but he did have a filthy white poodle that hated us. Joe was very ill with diabetes and the poodle guarded him from the foot of the bed, growling and snarling when we passed by the door. His dresser top was covered with safety-capped needles and prescription pill bottles. The following February my parents named my new little brother after Joe, who spent much of that winter in the hospital.

The photos from that year show a little girl, but no way did I feel like a little girl. The child in the photographs with a Dorothy Hamill haircut wore a dress in one shot, even as she climbed on a yellow tractor with her brother and sister. Other photos show that same girl in cut-off jeans and dirty T-shirt, two toads held in muddy hands. Two toads clasped tightly together.

Like most West Texas ranchers, we had a wet shack. When they first walked up, the illegal migrant workers rarely knocked on the ranch house door, but remained at the edge of the pasture, sending one of the group to the barn to wait until the men arrived. To wait for *el patron*. In return for their labor most ranchers furnished a bunkhouse, groceries, clothing from the River Ministry barrel at church, and enough cash for the men to go on down the road when they were ready or when the work ran out. Those men were walking toward their shaky American dreams, sending money home to their families. They were not dangerous in my memory. They just spoke a different language, and my father spoke enough Spanish to get by. My mother bought different groceries for them than she did to feed our family and the cowboys. I saved one of the plastic lard buckets and the next school year begged to use it as my lunch box rather than the more conventional one with Strawberry Shortcake on it.

That summer one of the Mexican men killed a rattlesnake and jerked it on the hood of the pickup truck in the hot afternoon sun. I sat with my chin on the scrubbed wooden table in their kitchen, watching them flip soft flour tortillas in a cast iron skillet. The bunkhouse always smelled of the propane cookstove and those tortillas. The room was melodious with the liquid of their language. When they handed me one of the folded tortillas, the warm butter that ran from between my fingers tasted better than the bright, cold margarine in our kitchen. But after my sister ate some of the rattlesnake, my mother forbade us to visit them again. I wish I had tasted that meat.

As summer aged, the shallow unexpected lakes slowly shrank in the sun and teemed with locked together couples that chorused through the night. Soon the puddles became gelatinous with eggs, then overcrowded with tadpoles in constant motion until they turned to black slime as August evaporated the water. We kids worked to save the tadpoles, filling our wading pool and the old plaster pond in the ranch house yard only to discover that it leaked. But we did manage to raise an admirable number of baby toads that hopped away like a moving carpet.

The August cicadas were loud in the trees on the afternoon my mother took me to the doctor in Carlsbad, New Mexico, to be treated for a urinary tract infection. As we drove home I got a lecture about cleanliness and dirty little girl fingers. The lecture was oddly juxtaposed with my mother's taking away the Tinkerbell bath set I had received as a birthday present that spring, saying the heavy perfume was not good for little girls.

Not too many years later I got a lecture about why good girls did not sit on boys' laps, did not put their girl parts next to a young man's boy parts, which was confusing to me because I had grown up sitting on laps, male laps, hard thighs under denim, pipe smoke or chewing tobacco and beer or coffee-smelling breath above, the tang of leather or horse or grease or cologne all around.

Today my job is all about sex. Here in these Arizona mountains, Gail manages a ranch primarily made up of land leased from the US Forest Service. He watches out always for the delicate riparian areas, the ephemeral creek bottoms where the water comes up in the fall and retreats downward in late spring to lie silent beneath the sand. We plan always for ovulation, copulation, fertilization, germination, conception, gestation, pollination, lactation. No one looks like a good manager without precipitation. After late winter or early spring rains, leopard frogs lay eggs in clusters and Arizona toads lay long jellied strings on the sunlit sandbars in the creeks.

Those clasped pairs are not really doing it. They are locked in *amplexus*, a pseudocopulation, an embrace for the purpose of fertilization employed by amphibians and limulids. Even now, my experience with both is limited. What do I know of horseshoe crabs or animals that dwell in the water? In the desert, only ample rainfall brings the toads up from beneath the soil where they've dug in to lie dormant, sometimes for years.

The male amphibian clasps the female around the middle so he is there. So he has a chance.

So he is present.

So when she lays her eggs, sitting there in his lap, his then-spilled seed will have a chance to fall upon them.

I collect a universe in Mason jars and line them up on my windowsill. Frog eggs in one jar, toad eggs in another. By mucking around in the edges of dirt tanks, I have discovered salamander eggs as well, teardrop-shaped sacks with small commas of life suspended inside. A third jar. After a few days, pond worms and algae sway above the mud in the bottoms of the jars, sway in a current that must be produced by the turn of the earth since my windowsill seems solid and still. Water bugs live and die in those small worlds, their life cycle continuing, no matter where. I look up the science and the vocabulary to lend legitimacy to my still-present penchant for playing in the mud, for my childish embrace of this natural world.

We all thought they were doing it—the frogs and toads of our child-hood summers.

Attending

In the Santa Maria Mountains of Arizona, the cows are hard to find. Most of the water is live rather than fed by windmills or wells or pipelines. When it rains the cows and the deer and the elk can drink almost anywhere there is a low spot, a basin, a *tinaja*. Animals lying under trees in the heat of the day leave no tracks.

The trees are only trees until I learn to see. Then they become shagbark cedar, alligator juniper, laurel, quinine, manzanita, oak of so many varieties that I have to keep looking them up in my plant book: white oak, Emory oak, shrub oak, live oak, turbinella, black jack, and gambel. In spring the rock echeveria blooms from beneath the boulders and the scent of ceanothus reminds me of a florist shop. In fall the buckthorn is heavy with dark-staining berries, and the mahogany is feathery with seeds. Just yesterday I saw a cow eating low-hanging mistletoe.

I am learning, when we trail up a group of cows, to see them, really see them. Catalog them in my mind. Three cows, two with calves, so that makes two pair and one dry cow . . . or is she bred, springing? Perhaps she's recently been to water and her belly is full. Two kicked-off yearlings, both branded, one a heifer, one a steer. A bull, one of the old Barzonas, #44. No longears in this bunch except for the two baby calves. I am not perfect at this cataloging yet. But every time we are in the sorting pen, I get better and my deep instinctual nature kicks in.

I had to explain to a magazine copy editor that yes, *malpais* really is a type of rock. Porous. Volcanic. Bad land. Bad dirt. And I know not only what it looks like but what it feels like against my skin, what it tastes like blown into my food, and what it smells like when my horse's shoes strike sparks against the holey stones. I look up at the horizon and silently name the landmarks: Rincon, Sheridan, BT Butte, Weber Canyon, Smith Mesa, Red Mountain, Castle Rock. We are riding single file, and I look back down at the trail just as Gail says, "Do you think we are going to jump that bear?" I bite my tongue before it blurts out, "What bear?" Sure enough, there in the powdery dust, right at my horse's feet, a smoking-hot bear track.

Dear God,
Please teach me to see.
Amen.

When I was a child, my father bought a blue and silver Chevy Suburban—drafty, unpadded, cavernous—perfect for four unbuckled children. On Tuesday nights we drove south of town to a home Bible study and on the way back, not only did the dark make it impossible to do homework or read a library book, but it also made us invisible.

Running along through the night, I heard my parents speak of a fellow Christian who had established a significant and growing ministry on the river.

The rio, rio grand, rio grande.

He collected clothes and food and medical supplies, hauled them down long dirt roads to people living in stick and adobe huts, often taking along volunteer doctors as he made his rounds. Baby doctors, eye doctors, a dentist. No one said their names aloud because it was illegal for them to tend to the people on the wrong side of that river, that muddy trickle.

But he'd stopped going to church.

Stopped attending.

He'd walked off from congregating town folks, started spending the Lord's Day with strangers who might not even be Protestant.

He took them food and prayers and songs.

Attending.

It was rumored that his favorite hymn wasn't even a hymn at all, but a Tom T. Hall song. In the darkness I could hear my parents' invisible head shakes and concern. What about the Body? What is Faith without Congregation?

Me and Jesus, we got our own thing going. Me and Jesus, we got it all worked out. Me and Jesus, we got our own thing going. We don't need no one to tell us what it's all about.

The highway sang beneath my head as I lay stretched out on the backseat.

Later on, my parents left the Baptist Church to become part of an even more fundamental group that preached the gospel from door to door.

Knocking on strangers' doors.

The summer I was sixteen we spent our Sunday mornings on the quiet brick streets of a neighborhood of old houses rented to university students, hoping to catch them at home so we could deliver our message using a pamphlet called *The Mystery of Human Life*. Inside its pages were diagrams showing the empty space inside each of us, the space meant only for God's dwelling. Indwelling.

One Sunday the air was so clear and the morning so near to perfect that I knew in advance what the afternoon would bring. Students would walk or ride their bikes all over this part of town, and the small community parks would fill with their laughter as they cooked on the grills, lay in the grass, and played sand volleyball. I envied their worn denim as I walked along the street in my straight skirt and prim blouse with the older brothers and sisters of our church. We'd risen early to pray over our morning's work.

At one house, grass grew up through the seams in the sidewalk. The chipped yellow paint on the plastered walls revealed a light teal beneath. A black sixties-era Mustang with red interior was parked in the driveway. We rang the doorbell but no one answered. As we waited to ring again, I looked through the low un-curtained window and saw a mound of blankets in the middle of the living room floor moving back and forth, back and forth, back and forth in rhythm.

I knew no one was going to answer that door, that there were other gospels for me, more mysteries within this human life, and I wanted to indwell them.

I love Sunday mornings more now than I ever did before. And I love the questions more than the answers.

Here on this ranch, we often sleep out when we are working cows. Days of the week mean less than the seasons. We take along a cast iron skillet, a roll-up table, a box of cooking supplies and canned goods, sometimes a cooler, a trailer full of number one alfalfa, a deck of cards and a cribbage board. Books. Wool stocking hats. Headlamps. Gail bought us a double-wide bedroll. We sleep beneath the stars, setting up a tent only if it looks like rain. We save our horses the round-trip trot to and from headquarters morning and evening. They hang out in camp with us. We eat with them. Sometimes they sleep, hip-cocked, a few feet from our heads.

On this Sunday morning we are camped up on Smith Mesa. We've been gathering cows into the trap here at Horseshoe Tank for three days. It rained all night as we lay in our mound of blankets, listening, celebrating, tent zipped. We always celebrate rain. The sun is still down behind the dam, but its early light is making jewels of the water standing in the soil between the *malpaís* rocks. My damp shirt smells of wind and sweat, wood smoke, cow manure, with a faint hint of propane from cooking breakfast on the camp stove since most of the wood is wet. I am sure I must have wiped my hands on the back of my jeans more than once. My boots are completely soaked, my spurs silenced by mud, my head snugged inside a wool beret while my felt cowboy hat hangs dripping in a tree. We are stuck in camp.

My hands are wrapped around a blue tin coffee cup, not for warmth so much as for happy while the cows move slowly down out of the trap above, coming to the hope of morning hay, content to leave their napping calves behind under a tree while the sun rises with such an intense beauty as to be a cliché, prosaic in its already-described colors.

Go ahead, the dawn beckons, try again, try to take my photograph, tell the world what you see, give words to my pink and my clouds.

Attend.

The old brown truck hooked to the green trailer is stuck immediately, its day's journey five feet long and a foot deep. We laugh ruefully as we saddle horses and drag the hay, one bale at a time, into the never-ending mud so we can cut the twine and toss flakes out in a circle. Recoil our muddy ropes.

Attendance. Our dance.

There are damp magazines on my damp pillow in my damp tent, one novel, and a book of poetry, materials to fill my day with words while the sun valiantly sucks water out of cow prints to make the mesa safer for our journey off and down. This process can't be rushed. We'll waste our day unplugged.

I dump a puddle out of a camp chair, stir some coals that steam in the shade, and scold a horse for nipping his neighbor. I will reach back and touch this shining morning when I lose it in the shadows.

Attending.

Three Crude Points

The moon set early tonight, sliding toward the west before the dark was even complete, but it wasn't much of a moon anyway, just a slim porcelain bowl, delicate, tired, leaving the party early.

There are three crude points, all made from the same green stone, all more ancient than you, lined up on the table in front of the fire. I know where each one came from, have a vivid memory of each finding, a catch in my throat and a triumph in my bones coupled with an abiding curiosity about the hands that knapped them, chose the soft green stone over another flint.

And my children break my heart a little bit at a time, don't you know, break little pieces of it off to hold on their tongues, tasting the sweet and the sour, the me who can't say yay or nay or kiss my ass because my throat is paralyzed with longing.

I have dreams, floor plans, whole books like ripe fruit within me, a distaste for plastic jewelry, ideals that fight to be lived, bashful poems, a lust for more intimacy. And yet, isn't intimacy the antithesis to lust?

Nonetheless, the moon set early tonight and made me think of building houses and hanging bits of colored glass from the ceilings, of growing mushrooms and knapping flint and dreams.

I mailed the package with his wedding ring in it, months after the divorce was final, and it slipped through the mail slot with an unromantic thunk, but I didn't have time to stand and salute or bow my head with grief.

The road home beckoned.

Aren't the Birds Pretty

My mother and I found the photo albums under the glass-topped coffee table in my grandparent's home, the house my grandfather built next door to his own father's house. Perhaps my grandmother's idea had been to make an album for each grandchild because there is one marked with my name and one with my sister's name. After that they become generic collections with many of the photographs showing my mother or my aunt or both pregnant, blonde-headed toddlers of various sizes around their feet. I am sure that to my very careful grandmother, the babies seemed to come awfully fast after the first two, three years apart.

That aunt is technically no longer my aunt, but we keep her anyway. The week my grandmother died, I thanked my re-married uncle for giving me two aunts rather than only one. If we were to fill a photo album with great-grandchildren, the heads would not all be blonde. I am envious that my youngest brother's children are growing up bilingual.

In my grandmother's lifetime, the idea of family moved and shifted and cracked and settled along ancient fault lines. After all, whose fault is it when love happens or blooms or dies or fades or changes? The bands of duty and obligation and propriety that bound my grandparents' generation popped and broke when the shifting sands of society caused family to be about heart and choice rather than blood and gender. Not better or worse, richer or poorer—just different.

Several times during the course of our turning the pages of the albums, my grandfather asked, "Where did these come from?" His own home is betraying him, spitting up its secrets. He held an album labeled *Reagan-Bush Era* with black magic marker on the cover.

My mother spoke about how my father's sister, another aunt, lamented that all three of her children had gotten divorces, thereby ruining her photo albums.

It was April 30, I forget the year. We rode out early of a morning after a big fight the night before. Working together means no time-out after hurtful words in the dark. I forget what we were fighting about. It takes a long time to get anywhere on this ranch, and hoof-falls and heartbeats are healing. The clouds were low to the earth, and as we climbed the ridge above Saddle Tank to look down into Smith Canyon, it seemed as if we became a part of them. As we stepped off to air our horses' backs before dropping down into the deep crease in the earth, a heavy late-spring snow began to fall all around us, one of the most beautiful moments of my life. Gail was riding Linda. I was riding Roscoe. Gail came around behind Linda and reached for my hands over Roscoe's enormous white rear. "Marry me, right here, right now." That is all the ceremony or certification we've ever needed. We had a party a few months later for our friends.

Dave Stamey sang "Come Ride With Me."

"We will make our families bigger instead of smaller." This was Gail's promise when we first got together, and now I see why. His family keeps everyone. When you're in, you're in. They don't dump anyone. Perhaps I've caught the same disease, or perhaps I am a result of this teenage millennium as I help my son's ex-girlfriend move into one of the family rent houses. My family felt smaller, though, when my daughter, Lily, chose a bedroom in my sister's home, two states away, so she could attend public high school. It was one thousand miles to drop her off, sign papers to make her safe in case of an emergency, and one thousand miles back. Those thousand miles were harder than any divorce.

My daughter is friends with Gail's stepdaughter with his first wife, Juanita. The other stepdaughter adopted a precious little boy and the birth mother ate Thai food with us the day after his first birthday. We are grandparents now. All of the river trip gear is stored in Juanita's basement, and I borrowed her boat for my first trip down the San Juan. After my daughter moved to college, my ex-husband moved into her bedroom—the one in my sister's house. Gail's sister married a man who used to be married to . . . never mind. Check the box that says, *It's complicated.*

Of course it is hard, especially around the holidays. We don't always want to be bigger. It was hard at the beginning when I sat on the couch by the woodstove while Gail went to town on Christmas Eve, smoothing the way for my eventual inclusion in future celebrations. His eyes looked so sad when he finally came back through the door. His sister told me, during our first meeting, "I am Switzerland." Like swimming through jellyfish. We all play poker together on New Year's Eve.

We eat our meals at the table Juanita made out in the wood shop at the Chino Valley homestead with Gail's ex-stepfather's help. It's too big for her new house in town, but someday she will reclaim it. Gail's son cut a load of firewood that is still in our garage until he finds a pickup to haul it to his house in a college town. I do not feel like a stepmother; after all, he has many mothers already. Gail's brother's ex-girlfriend still lives in his back bedroom. Their cat died and we'll catch one of the barn kittens soon, take it to town to fill the empty space. I never had a stepparent, and I listen with envy when Gail speaks of all that his stepparents added to his life. His ex-stepmother signs her notes to me on Facebook with *The Wicked One*. Gail says she is the one who taught him to work, picking up rocks out of the arena, blanketing horses, hauling buckets of water. He speaks of her with love.

Everyone in Gail's family has little people on our shelves, cunning figurines made of Sculpey, a polymer clay, baked and hardened. They are decorated with costume jewelry or polished rocks or shells or beads. Their round benevolence and welcoming presence in everyone's home offered continuity when I couldn't keep all the relationships straight. The tower where Gail's mother created them is round, a workshop built especially for her by her then-husband and her sons. It is made of pounded earth and adobe. I stand in the middle of it, and in that place I can imagine a full and beautiful life where there are no bad guys.

I cosigned for my son Oscar's truck and he wrecked it almost immediately. Lily has wrecked two vehicles, and since Gail has had much experience with stepdaughters I liked hearing him tell her, "A good wreck is one where nobody gets hurt." She tells me on the phone that everyone, from the man whose car she hit to the policeman who wrote the citation to the insurance adjuster, has been too nice and she wishes someone would yell at her. So I do. I tell her that I can't imagine living in a world where she does not breathe and to slow down and stop *shooting the gap*, whatever that means. When I pause to catch my own breath, she says, "Ok, you can stop yelling now." I am going to ask my mother-in-law for one of her little people to put in Lily's dorm room.

Stepparenting is one thing. Coparenting is quite another. Sharing Lily with my sister, Molly, and her husband, Paul, has been a huge blessing with barbs. Molly has two children from a previous marriage, and Paul has two children of his own, so the blended family is five kids—oddly related—steps and cousins and true siblings all mixed up in the pot of one floor plan. Jessica and Wayne are brother and sister, and Lily is their cousin. Julie and David are brother and sister. Lily and Julie look alike but do not share one drop of blood. Socially they all refer to each other as siblings. When we first stirred them together, it looked like a mob that would last forever, but university campuses keep taking bites. Next year Molly and Paul will come home from work to an empty house on the days when Wayne is at his father's. He's the last child at home. But there will be evenings when my ex-husband isn't at work.

It's all complicated. And all relative.

I have lived with angry men all of my life, and yes, I look at myself as the common denominator in the equation. At least when they are yelling at me, I know I exist. My father taught me that men are angry. Or hilarious. Or reclusive. Or however they choose to be in the world, with few repercussions. The loudest person wins.

Once, during a meal, when he was angry again, we all sat in stiff silence, hoping not to draw his anger our way. My mother, always and forever trying to make peace, looked out the plate glass window and said, "My, aren't the birds pretty." Fortunately, my father was teetering, maniacally, on the edge where he could either pound the table and roar with anger or pound the table and roar with laughter at this ridiculous non sequitur. He roared, this time, with laughter.

My mother's sentence has become part of our family lore. I often re-interpret it to mean, *Ignore what is too unpleasant to face head on.* So, we don't talk about tattoos or my nose bling or her ruined picture albums or where we keep the marriage certificates.

Using Tools Backwards

In the shadow of Jones Mountain, we are tearing down the old white house. Bright curtains no longer flutter when the breeze blows through broken windows. Toys no longer lie abandoned on the floor. A plaque asking us to "Bless This House" no longer hangs above the mantle of a cold hearth where fires no longer burn. A coffee pot no longer bubbles in the kitchen; no bedsprings creak in the night. Water no longer gushes from the faucets, booted feet no longer stomp on the porch, and potted geraniums no longer bloom on the sills.

Weather started the process after everyone moved on to newer homes with modern architecture, busier lives, easier climates, so that the seasons pass unannounced, unnoticed, uncelebrated within these walls. The only sign of life is a swallow swooping out of a window the moment a human foot scrapes the floor. Sunlight filtering through a rain-stained hole in the ceiling lays waste to whatever hope there once was that this house would breathe again.

We are tearing down the old white house—stripping off the roof, ripping off the siding, removing the door frames. Piling up heavy, old-fashioned window weights. Exposing pipes and uncovering secrets. We find a bird's nest, cunningly hidden in the wall, and move it with its straining, chirping inhabitants to a place up under some rafters we are leaving for now, a good place for bird babies to finish growing.

We are tearing down the old white house, a job the boss has been talking about for years. It wasn't hurting anything for the structure to slowly give way to gravity and weather, but a clerk with the county searched on Google Earth and saw it, actually saw it, from her desk in the city. She asks for dollars, dollars, yearly dollars, property taxes on a home built before there was a never-ending price to pay for keeping rain and snow and wind out of one's frying pans. Dollars per square foot. Numbers attached to numbers.

There is a cave on the side of Jones Mountain, one with drawings on the walls, black on the ceiling, and pottery sherds on the floor. I wonder if the clerk can see that dwelling place on her map, and if there would be any tax on living there, any paperwork or inspections, anyone to care if I dug a hole in the dirt floor to contain my fire, any numbers that mattered. Perhaps it is the only place left one can live where only the wild things would come to visit. I find myself wanting to look up the word *habitable*.

In the shadow of Jones Mountain, I am learning to use tools backwards. The full-dimension Douglas fir lumber is meant to be stacked until we build our own house. Someday. In the July heat, it is hard for me to believe in someday houses. Before I came here, I had never lived anywhere longer than five years, but out of hope and bullheadedness I am pulling nails instead of pounding them. Using a flat bar instead of a measuring tape. Discovering the marvels of an impact driver instead of a screwdriver. Un-shingling instead of shingling, unwiring, un-plumbing.

And I am left cold.

But enthusiasm is like the moon, and as soon as it wanes it begins to wax anew.

In the shadow of Jones Mountain, we are tearing down *her* house. As the destruction reveals the construction, I touch something of humanity.

She comes alive for me.

I know that there is no *she*, that many women lived here through the years, many women put their special touches on this house; many women stored milk in the cellar, hung beeves from the high hooks, planted gardens, swept the floors, raised babies, stood in the wind while pinning laundry to dry. But as I work, I begin to talk to her, to that collage-woman, the woman I have created in my mind, the one who lived here in the shadow of Jones Mountain, longer than five years.

We could not have pushed or burnt or moved this house, a fact we discover gradually as the original cabin is revealed, unveiled from beneath modern materials and improvements, sitting patiently in the center of several additions. A French-style vertical log structure made of hand-hewn pine and cedar tree trunks sunk into the ground, chinked with mud, a stark cube that must have been dark and cold.

Lonely.

Fifteen feet by seventeen feet.

Suffocating.

I carry a camera in my pocket every day, especially after I find the newspapers tacked beneath the siding.

From the *Bellingham Herald*, spring 1909:

Help Wanted—Female: Refined young man of good habits desires the acquaintance of lady 27 years to 29, one who is matrimonially inclined; no triflers need apply; photograph returned upon approval.

I ask her . . . did you come here from somewhere far away over a hundred years ago? Did you think this creek bottom below Jones Mountain was beautiful or desolate or both? Did you plant the apple trees, the pear?

Did you despair to hold your firstborn by the woodstove while the wind whistled between the logs in December? Were you reluctant or eager to bring those old newspapers out of your trunk, giving up your precious words to line the outer walls, warmth having become more important than holding on to the past? I hope you dreaded the coming winter less as the men nailed up the tongue-and-groove siding hauled in by wagon over long roads you rarely got to travel.

We are hauling the old white house to the city dump over those same roads, shattered pieces in a trailer that rattles and hums on the pavement.

I barely breathe, keeping my mouth tightly locked and my nostrils sucked inward as we tip the trailer to unload. The beep beep beeeeep of heavy machinery never stops. It rises above the sounds of glass and wood and sloppy wet bags hitting the asphalt while the bigger-than-a-house Caterpillar pushes and slides the piles of detritus from a consumer society into a truck trailer parked below ground. A man wears a bright orange vest as he rummages through the garbage, making sure the most precious commodity, cardboard, gets pulled out and set aside. I wonder if his beard catches the stench of this place the way I know my hair is catching the dust of so much squandered junk. I wonder how the worker keeps from getting depressed, and I want to know that he takes a shower *first thing* when he gets home, washing off the weight of this place.

I am embarrassed by the volume of my own garbage. The man parked next to us tosses a television out of his truck, plastic housing and glass screen shattering on the concrete.

We are hauling her house to the city dump, one piece at a time.

And I ask her so many things. How did you fit onto the map, and what did it look like in your head? How could I ever explain to you why your roof is visible from outer space?

Did you hate or love the blank white sheetrock after it was nailed up over the 1x6 boards you had lovingly papered in a dark green patterned cloth? I want you to know that I saved a scrap of it, for you brought beauty to this place.

You were not alone here. As I peel away the improvements, I find pack rat nests, scorpions, black widows, stashes of walnuts and juniper berries and acorns, evidence of squirrels and uninvited visitors. I find the dehydrated bodies of dead creatures and hope that when they were bloated and decaying in these walls, it was not August, that you were not pale with morning sickness, that you didn't have houseguests from back East gagging in mid-afternoon with the stench you could not locate nor extricate.

Did you welcome the rustle and squeak of the bats up under the eaves or did you cry at night?

In the shadow of Jones Mountain, the rock chimney now stands alone, at the edge of what must have been your new room added onto the cabin, wood floors replacing the hated and hateful dirt that got into every pot of soup, every fold of every garment. The red brick extension atop the rock rises up into the sky, and I wonder how long you had to complain about the smoke blowing back down into your new parlor until the extra bricks were added.

And did you hold your breath with delight when they enclosed the front porch to make a bathroom, bringing the plumbing indoors? And the wall heaters! As I unwire and unbolt them from the walls, even one in the kitchen, I wonder if you reveled in their clean heat, in the utter luxury of it all.

All of this will soon be gone, for we are leaving only the original square cabin, the one that cries out *history!* We cannot bear to raze its heavy logs. The tax assessor has scheduled a trip over the long dirt road to make sure that it is not *habitable.*

Do you know that your house makes me sad? With a crowbar, I pry up the new countertop in the kitchen and find the old one, ancient linoleum stuck to wood with black tar, a large round burned mark where someone (damn him) set a hot skillet. I find your son's toys, faded metal trucks and cars, lost deep in the woodwork, behind heavy built-in flour and potato bins, and I wonder if he cried.

I stop with my prying and hammering and destructing and stand looking up at Jones Mountain. What did you do with your silence? Did you try to fill it every moment of every day? Did you sing and hum and scream and, finally, when the wires came, plug in a radio? Or did you stand, as I am, and allow the silence to collapse in on itself, fill itself with the wind through the cottonwoods along the creek, the piñon jay's bossy voice, the lowing of a cow coming along the bottoms?

I hope you had a windmill for company.

In the shadow of Jones Mountain, we are tearing down your house.

Ugly Mud Bugs

The ugly mud bugs live deep in the black smelly muck at the bottom of the water trough. They are creepy prehistoric-looking insects that burrow into the sulfurous primordial ooze and scatter their papery exoskeletons around the edges. Most people never even notice their existence except maybe the children who squish their toes in the creek bottoms. These bugs are not good to eat, and there is no money to be made on their sheds, no reason to pay them much attention. The ugly mud bugs can live in the mire for up to five years. During this time, they molt over and over again, shedding tired old crackly skin for fresh tender new skin before disappearing back down into the murk.

Once, during a murky time of my own, I stood beside the Virgin River in Zion National Park, looking up at the cliffs that make that place famous, cradling a warm cup of coffee in my hands. I had been camping alone, though in a public campground, for several days with several more to go. On that early morning, as I watched, a rock slide started near the top of one of the cliffs and rolled halfway down the side of the face, taking huge trees, tons of dirt, and boulders as big as houses to new resting places. It was as if I was watching a silent movie, and it happened with an almost unbelievable speed. I don't know if anyone else in the campground that morning saw it, and though I listened all day, I never heard anyone comment on the event. It was way over our heads.

The next day I joined a group of nine strangers for a hike through Left Fork on a route known as The Subway. One of the organizers of the hike had recognized my Texas accent in a restaurant in Kanab, Utah. He was a fellow Texan and offered me the leftover spot on a hike that requires both a permit and that someone in the group have knowledge of, and gear for, technical climbing.

I don't like group activities.

I am terrified of heights.

I don't like cold water.

I have no idea, even now, why I agreed to go, why I signed on, why I crawled out of my tent in the early morning and met the group by the backcountry ranger's desk in the visitors' center. Perhaps twelve days of solitude loomed or perhaps leaving behind all I had ever known, travelling solo, finding my way through the murk did not seem adventurous enough. Who knows why we say yes?

That day I found myself sitting in a strange man's lap as we did a tandem descent since I was too scared to rappel alone. I found myself swimming in very deep, very cold water. I found myself celebrating over Mexican food with the group at the end of the day. Beers all around.

Historically, when human beings have made big changes, left behind old ways and sought new sunrises, they've done so for ideals, for concepts bigger than themselves like freedom, independence, strength, survival, adventure, and opportunity. The storytellers of all time have found those words hard to weave into legend; instead they ask the eagle and the bear and the buffalo and the mountain lion to carry them, metaphors being more powerful than flags and documents and councils.

Even now, when many of the wild places in the American West have been paved over or cut through or plowed under or fenced in, the very best metaphors for our lives are found when we step out of our houses and offices, when we get out of our cars and schedules, when we lace up our shoes and seek out a trail, a tree, a creek.

Deep in thousands of unknown, unnamed canyons of the West, water seeps from between the rocks, wild roses bloom, squirrels come to drink, as do snakes, javelina, deer, skunks, and juncos. They grow and they die; they eat and they play; they breathe and they fight and they burrow for winter, and it all happens whether we are there to see it or not.

A pair of zone-tailed hawks come to the same tree year after year to raise their young, and they scream at us as we ride beneath the nest . . . we call it music.

The West captures the imaginations of those of us who treasure the wild things, those who ache for wide skies, independent wings, sheer rock faces, for lives that are hardy and un-tamable. The West snags us with too-big landscapes as well as with minute details that have hooks in them, with science that leads to art, with old places, and new, with places that echo with the past by flinging pieces of broken pots at our feet. We cling to the knowledge that if we desire to, that if we venture out of the insulated boxes where we live, we can know when the water comes up in the fall, sinks down in the spring, when the cast of characters changes with the sunset and the season. We revel in the fact that there are so many details we must train ourselves to see, so many places we must go and stand on real dirt.

The manzanita blooms and tastes like honey. The lizards do push-ups on the rocks. Bears leave barefoot tracks on cow trails, and hummingbirds do rain dances in August. Storms blow up and lightning strikes. Sometimes the snow is so heavy that ancient oaks crack under its weight. The whole desert gives the Gila monster the right-of-way, and rarely do we get our cameras out fast enough. In spring a vermilion flycatcher displays from atop a fence post, making himself visible in the opposite direction from his dull mate sitting on her nest. Go ahead. Admire his brilliant feathers. And so, the metaphors pile up around us; we are invited to fall in love every day.

During that time of transition when I stood and watched the rock slide in Zion, I was faced with many choices. I could have gone back to college and applied for a *real* job. I could have gone back to my husband and tried to put our dutiful family back together, but instead I sought out the wild places. And now I know that it is because I must be here when that ugly mud bug, the one who swims and molts and burrows in the smelly black silt, finally crawls up out of the primordial ooze. I must be here when on that perfect day she climbs up out of the mud, reaches for the sun, balances herself on a reed or the side of the trough and, one last time, splits her exoskeleton neatly down the back, and emerges. Emerges into the sunlight in iridescent glory, no longer an ugly mud bug, but a jewel-toned dragonfly.

Like a Raccoon Peeking In

~for Fred and Rusty

Sometimes it pays to leave the ranch.

Seagulls at dawn as I wait for the alarm remind me that I am not in my place. So I listen. We go on journeys to learn new stories.

As a documentary filmmaker in addition to ranch foreman, Gail goes on interesting journeys, and this week he is working on a video project in San Francisco. I have come along as second camera, a new role in a new setting with a new way of seeing. The writer observes, but through the lens of passionate reflection. The camera records exactly what is—missed opportunities cannot be painted in and mistakes in framing or content cannot be edited out. I cannot use my imagination. I either get it on film or I don't.

Turn the camera on when you get there, turn it off when you leave. Tape is cheap.

We're rolling.

We meet a man who makes me think about sound. He can tune a rubber band, bring a baby or a dog or an explosion into our midst, evoke cicadas from our childhood treetops, creating summer for each person in the room. He can make a board break with a Styrofoam picnic plate. And he can sing.

He says, "If the movie scares you, turn the volume down. The images you are seeing are only data, information. It is the sound that evokes the emotion."

We sit on the floor of a hotel room beneath an Andy Warhol print, drinking Irish whiskey over ice and speaking of metaphor, storytelling, bearing witness, tequila. We speak of our parents and grandparents and children. We speak this night of our work. It is affirming to be in the presence of those who love their work and that is part of the gift I will take home with me. The sound-maker tells of making the sounds of Old Faithful, of recording tectonic plates shifting miles beneath the surface of the earth, of rubbing two slabs of granite together and then dropping it eight octaves. I tell of my grandfather's horse stories, remembered gestures and words. The carpet on which we sit is stiff and rough; there are purple roses on the print above us. At the same time, we both see the raccoon peeking in the window by the door. In almost any other setting, it would simply have been a really cool sighting. But we are in the Phoenix Hotel in the heart of San Francisco, in the Tenderloin district among skyscrapers, apartment buildings, streetcars, concrete, traffic, and grocery carts.

One of my best friends is totally deaf, locked inside himself by tumors that continue to rob him of the swirl of life. Without sound, his world is reduced to data. He sees the stream, but does not find the burbling peace. He sits on the front porch of an evening, but does not hear the mosquito singing in his ear or the frogs stroking the night with love calls or the crickets eating apricots in the trees. He no longer has songs to rock his blood. He doesn't hear the catch in his mother's voice when she tells of the doctor's latest e-mail saying there is nothing more to be done to stop the silently growing tumors.

Where do his cries go in the night when he is all alone? For truthfully, his is not a world without emotion, but rather a world without the tempering of his own feelings by the emotions of others. He is a raccoon peeking in.

I am learning to listen, to listen to stories rather than focusing on my own. Rather than deciding what I am going to say next. I am learning to listen to her story and his story and your story . . . all the stories as they are told. The swirl and music of story. We tell our stories from when we were children dodging the upheaval of adults. We tell our stories from young adulthood, editing as we go. We tell our stories of pain and happy and fear and tequila and child rearing. We tell about raccoons peeking in surprising windows.

One morning in San Francisco I stepped over a puddle of vomit on my way to a breakfast of crawfish beignets and chicory coffee. San Francisco sirens sound different from sirens in other cities. They have different stories. I heard the murmur of the women sitting in unaccustomed sun, braiding hair into cornrows, gossiping with people who walked by. They were telling stories. I found myself wishing I could hear the fog—wishing my ears could, indeed, hear the sounds of *little cat feet*. That evening I saw a streetcar go by, but the moment was lifted up out of the ordinary, the data, the information . . . not by the sparks that flew from the insulators at the intersection so much as the accompanying *zippft zippft*. The sound. Later I heard a steel guitar and watched the flash of the player's rings as her fingers zipped along the strings. Her stories are in her hands.

When we return to the ranch, to our mountains, the idea of soundtrack stays with me. The snake that rattles and hisses when Gail's horse steps off the trail to turn a cow back no longer seems evil, but natural. He is offering warning. We came to his house, and he's allowed to tell his story. I ride on the North Benches and imagine the silhouette of a bronze brave high on the rim rock above me. Without Hollywood to write the music, would his presence seem ominous or protective, threatening or benevolent? I ache with having missed his time here in this place, ache with having missed his story.

Hollywood gives us soundtracks for lovemaking, too. For sex scenes. No squishing or skin slapping on skin. No unscripted moans and chirps. Nothing messy. No honest dirty talk—just love talk, love words. The music is orchestrated strings in composed movements, and percussion.

I am back in my office and rain begins falling outside my window. Visually, nothing has changed. My desk faces the blank wall. The words are still black and white on the page, but emotionally, everything has changed. Rain . . . on an Arizona cow outfit in mid-September. Gentle rain to aid the grass's growing on into the fall. Rain to fill up the dirt tanks and water catchments and granite basins. Rain to nurture winter fodder for the cows and the peace we've been seeking. I would not have known that the rain had begun to fall had not the sound reached me through the open window long before the smell of wet oakbrush and duff crept in. The sound reaches me and changes my mood, my perception of the day, changes my concentration. Like a raccoon peeking in.

Mad Money

We were ranch wives, living in shitty little camp houses at the ends of long dirt roads that were slick when it was wet, dusty when it was dry and sometimes both in one afternoon. We were stretching paychecks that put us below poverty level according to the government because the IRS hadn't figured out how to count housing, beef, and utilities as income at tax time. Still, $900/mo doesn't stretch very far when you're feeding growing children.

We were hungry. Not just hungry for the fancy cheeses and intriguing deli selections at the new supermarket that even had a salad bar. We learned the hard way that boiled eggs weigh too much when buying salad-by-the-pound, even as a treat on shopping day. But we didn't shop at places like that anyway. We drove on past, headed to the Super Wal-Mart and Sam's Club to spend $300 on food for thirty days. We poured the top two inches out of gallons of milk and put them in the freezer. We thought carefully about every single item we put in our carts and resented the months when we had to buy a new bale of toilet paper. I bought cheap-ass toilet paper. Once, as I turned east along the interstate to drive the eighty miles back out to the ranch, I cried because I had not bought the $7 bottle of Neutrogena sesame bath oil . . . but by god we had toilet paper.

We were hungry for happy.

Most of us didn't have jobs because we lived too far from town, so we schemed about ways to pad our incomes. Someone was always coming up with a new idea, or at least it sounded new to us. Many of us had jars or hidden places in our sock drawers where we stashed the occasional dollar bill, or if we were lucky a five, or if we'd just gotten a birthday card from our parents, a bigger, more delicious amount.

One of us was always hosting a party of some sort. Home Interiors was very popular for a while, especially when they came out with a Western line. Our husbands made fun of the lack of authenticity in the print of some guy riding away in soft gold light and a cheap frame. The collections made our living rooms look like hotel rooms. Mary Kay Cosmetics was good for about two parties a year, but none of us ever drove a pink Cadillac. And then there were all those candle parties, and then that jewelry company for a while, and those really expensive, but handcrafted, baskets. They looked Amish. We got a meal at the cookware parties though we went home to our trusty cast iron and wedding present CorningWare. At the packaged food parties, the dips all tasted the same. I'd page through each catalog that came with the invitation, searching for the least expensive item since I usually had about $34 of mad money in the drawer, if that. For those who signed up to host a party, there were hostess gifts in levels tied to how many dollars your guests spent. I never hosted a party though, because my dirt road was one of the longest.

We were so young. Perhaps the parties were our excuse to get dressed up and make our husbands watch the kids for the evening. We'd drive down dirt roads to connect with other dirt roads and stand around eating whatever finger food the hostess had worked all day to prepare—strawberries dipped in white fluff, little sausages marinated in equal parts grape jelly and yellow mustard in the slow cooker, baby carrots dipped in ranch dressing, lemon chess bars, brownies from a box. We complained about our men and the weather and the cost of gasoline. The salesperson seemed so glamorous bustling around setting up her displays, but really, she was just another ranch wife hoping we'd make her evening worthwhile. She'd give her presentation and try to convince us to sign up to be on her "team." These things were always pyramid schemes. Multi-level marketing. If you worked hard enough, you got big paychecks. The American dream, one party at a time.

We lusted after the stuff. If only our candles could sit in seasonal holders and our walls have specific arrangements, including the sconces, if only we had the Day's End Blue eye shadow, if only I could redecorate my bedroom in a safari theme, if only my apples rested in the basket with the green-checked liner and the yellow-check could wait folded in the drawer for when I needed a change . . . then it would all be better. Then I would be *happy*. Then I wouldn't care about buying toilet paper instead of bath oil, even in winter. At the end of the evening, we'd carefully fill out our order forms. $34 + tax.

to the man who sings . . .

~for Gail

Just a collection of cells, arranged into a pinhead body with eight legs, trapped in the dry white bathtub, doomed to be crushed in a tissue and flushed away because our culture deems the collection scary or creepy, possibly even dangerous.

Just a collection of cells, arranged into green leaves that wilt in hot butter, and we add garlic and lemon juice, more collections of cells to feed our own.

Just a collection of cells, arranged miraculously to crow and lay and peck and strut, protein structures that walk around on clawed feet.

Just a collection of cells, precious as you sleep by my side, but no more or less important than the collections of cells that bark in the night or hoot and call down in the creek or sink roots in the garden or grow heavy with calf or weave a web or slither with uninterrupted backbone.

Just a collection of cells arranged into so many intricate designs, some to pump blood, some to store fat, some to grow hair, some to turn calories into motion.

. . . and yet you sing.

Willow Springs

I have been riding toward Willow Springs my whole life.

When we first began to correspond, Gail wrote to me about going to Willow and how he imagined my going with him some day. He wrote of dragging a mattress out onto the porch to sleep during the hot nights of summer, of taking a shower at the windmill using a solar bag hanging from the struts. He joked about it being just another cow camp full of mouse shit.

I answered his e-mail from a wall tent in the eastern Sierras. "Are there really willows at Willow Springs?" He answered yes, yes there really are willows around the springs. He also explained that years ago his boss told him to cut them down because they interfered with the windmill, from both above and below ground. Gail found ways to delay that job, an act of anarchy. That boss's ashes are scattered down in the desert where his own grandfather homesteaded, but a faded painting of him riding a bucking horse overlooks all our meals. The willows still grow. They are enormous now, their roots sunk deep.

I have been riding toward Willow Springs my whole life. And the reason for my question, long before I followed Gail, twelve miles on horseback, to this remote camp in the lower part of the ranch, is that there are many places in the West named Willow Springs, and not all of them have willows left, not all of them have water left. Not all of them have western aquatic garter snakes and leopard frogs or vermilion flycatchers.

It is just a simple cabin on a national forest, no electricity or running water, jersey sheets on the bed, a wrench always by the front door after we hook up the propane bottle so we can cook, bird nests and flint chippings on the windowsills, small forgotten pieces of everything piled every-where, evidence of solitary nights spent here before me. Eleven-year-old newspapers and faded *Western Horseman* magazines. Bits of leather and twine. A dry-rotted cinch hanging from a nail. Needles and matches in an ashtray. Half-empty whisky bottle on a bottom shelf and a cast iron skillet hanging from a nail. A jerky line stretched overhead. In the saddle shed is an old wooden cabinet with the names of cowboys carved into its doors, fifty years of men who have cowboyed on the Spider and slept at Willow Springs. I haven't carved my name there yet.

Sometimes I ride the quad to Willow Springs the day before we ride in on horses. On the quad trail, it's two hours in, two hours back out. I leave behind a cooler with ice and meat, sometimes cheese and bacon and eggs, lettuce. We eat well those first few days and have two nights' ice for our toddy. After that we eat out of cans until we head for home. I look forward to some of those later meals—the chicken and corn chowder, perhaps the steakhouse chili. Gail's favorite is corned beef hash, fried crisp in a hot skillet.

We deal cribbage hands by headlamp, cuss cell phone batteries, then turn everything off while he plays music in the dark. We hauled the gui-tar in one day last summer, with the cooler and the meat. It lives here now, a cheap guitar, one that wouldn't be a big loss if it accidentally walked off. After we return to headquarters, that guitar, left behind to hang silent on the wall, becomes my talisman of songs yet to come, nights yet to come, days at Willow Springs yet to come.

Few Americans will experience six days in a row without ice or a shower, will know a week without cell phone or computer or Miracle Whip, will understand how Jupiter can become a friendly face or how to wash dishes with a paper towel and leftover coffee in a camp with no running water. At least we have coffee.

If the wind is blowing, we set the five-gallon water container beside the windmill to fill and hope the horses don't knock the pipe off. When it is full we slip an ax handle beneath the plastic loop in the top and each lift a side to carry it to the cabin. Gail often mentions how many times he awkwardly staggered to the house with a heavy fiver of water before I got here. I like it that I am here now, to lift my end of things.

Going to Willow Springs is hard work—not just what we do when we are there, but the actual getting there—is hard work. The boatmen on the Colorado River say that it takes three full days to fully unplug from life and from the media and even from this thing we call reality—except perhaps when we turn off the juice and go to the wild, we don't leave reality so much as sink that much further into it—so that to reach the surface level of news feed and ringtones once more, we must push off the restful bottom and kick hard. At Willow Springs we work, but when we get to the cabin at clock-less time, we drink a beer, breathe, look at the shelves until a can of whatever catches our eye. We open the windows or build a fire, check for scorpions in the bedding before the sun goes down, light the pilots on the stove. But no hurry. There are chores, sure, and sunsets, and we might see a cow up there on the trail around the top of the horse pasture—guess we'll pick her up tomorrow on our way to Sheridan. The most pressing question as the sun goes full down is who will win at cribbage tonight. We keep a yearly tally. The loser is in charge of planning the next year's Valentine's Day celebration.

No one tells us what to think or what time the sun will shine tomorrow—and while the world still spins, rocks us in time to its circle of light and dark, the noise of nonsense is miles away, trapped by electronics that have no power here. Our weather comes over the ridges. The newscaster is old #16, broadcasting his arrival at the spring with bellows that sound gentle in the night compared to a siren or a bulletin. Just a bull, looking for love. Our need for entertainment does not diminish as the cheap guitar plays familiar chords under Gail's fingers—but we are delighted by subtle things now, things highlighted, brought forward by the deficit, no longer obscured by an artificial stream designed to keep me from getting bored—no, wait—designed to make me dissatisfied so that I might purchase something new.

I have never brought money to Willow Springs. Or the wallet of cards embossed with too many names and numbers. The stray pennies in the ashtray are lost here. We are resting in reality, where the silence is cacophony—the plot is life and death—the momentous is that big steer who voluntarily jumped over the fence to eat hay with the cows. Where fatigue and rest means muscles and work.

With my attention no longer enslaved, I see the wasp galls on the oaks, slit them open with my thumbnail to find the embryo inside. I notice what is growing, seeding, moving among the rocks. Wheeling high overhead. I see my lover's face change and shift with his thoughts. Oh, that someone would see me so clearly, without a media, social overlay.

"Bill Murphy sent me in here for the winter . . . I think it was '81. He told me to gather all the cows out of the Granites and take them down to the Basin. Cut the bulls out and put them in the lower horse pasture at Willow. That's how I learned to trail up cattle, to handle cattle. You learn a lot about moving cattle when you have to do it all by yourself."

He had four or five horses, a guitar, an old Power Wagon, and books. When he went to town every few weeks for groceries, he'd stop at the used book store on Gurley Street and trade in those he'd read, pick out another sackful. Town was Prescott, Arizona. That was when the old cabin still had running water and a truck would still come out to fill the propane tank. He wrote songs.

"Those cows would go good. Once we got to the bottom of Smith Canyon, they'd climb out the other side onto the South Benches and pretty much go on their own. The bulls though . . . they didn't want to go up that steep-ass hill to Willow. I remember one old lump-jawed Angus bull . . . I fought him for two hours back and forth between two trees. If I'd had a gun with me, I would have shot him."

Today we made a fourteen-mile circle under hot blazing sun, a long day of seeing only old sign. There were no fresh tracks, no fresh shit, just critter prints on the trails. The cows have moved out of this country. The heat drove them to cooler canyons and up onto a mesa with breezes. We sit on the porch with lukewarm beers and say, "Well, we know where they are not . . ."

Ten hours in the saddle and what did August serve up?

Bull-rubbed baby cedars and sun-ripe prickly pear fruits, heated through and strung together with cicada song.

Dry empty nests serenaded from above by suddenly freed parents, feathers ruffled, and now the small rumble of thunder silences us all. The lizards are fat with eggs for spring and barely move from the rocktops as we ride by. Quail sisters gossip in the shade of oakbrush.

Ants build hopeful hills, taking seeds out to act as sponges, and when I pull my saddle off, my sweat is so mixed with horse sweat that I can't tell the difference; my knees ache.

Almost-empty beer in hand, I stand in the breeze in soaked tank top as the windmill slowly squeaks with the storm's turn, and he says, "That thing sounds like Jimi Hendrix!"

Tonight we will sleep beneath a waning moon. Tonight we will sing together, old songs and new. Loudly, we sing. Softly, we sing. One of the songs has a lyric about being scared of falling off into the sky, but I'm not afraid.

Ezekiel 33:10b, KJV . . .
how should we then live?

Cardboard sign, old and bent, says "friend for life 25 cents."
When did this start making sense? Man, it's really getting cold.
~Guy Clark, "Homeless"

You determine to recycle, do unto others, leave no trace except an acceptable work of art, minimize your footprint, smile at a stranger because he might be having a bad day, yield when the sign says to, even when it is your turn, waving your neighbor on by. You purchase wisely, eat thoughtfully, grow spinach, put out the positive energy that you want to receive back, remember with each breath that love is, indeed, the thing . . . until you decide that it might be kindness. You give the homeless man at the convenience store $5 because the wind is so cold, and who cares how and why he got there. You'll sweep your own porch first.

But then, well, you watch the emissions build, the planet gasp, the children starve and bleed, the nuclear reactors leak, the rudeness swirl, the old people sit on curbs with cups and signs, the beer store right around the corner. The news feed is guns and police brutality and racial tension and politics-as-entertainment and one percent and there is no one representing me. The popular songs become unintelligible, the night sky becomes soiled, the consumers become unaware of what they consume as pink slime and aspartame and GMOs gain support on a congressional floor that no longer upholds honor or freedom but is polluted by dollars, meaning-less ones and zeros. Brad gives Angie a $500,000 ring.

How then shall I live my life?

I catch my monthly flow in flannel pads and soak them in a basin, squeeze them clean, pour the bloody water on the tree of life in my garden. The tree bears fruit one season at a time, and it is a mystery fruit that only tastes sweet when the moon is full.

In Lieu of Flowers

Fort Stockton, Texas, March 2011

"God gave us the gift of dead dinosaurs and all of the animals that died in the flood, and we need the government to let us do more drilling."

He'll be ninety in September, and his eyes get wet when he tells us this part of West Texas hasn't had any moisture for over 150 days. He's lived here all his life. His own father's heart was broken when the irrigation water dried up. From then until the end of his life, he sat on the porch and grouched and swatted flies.

"God only left eight people alive on the earth, you know."

He gazes down a seven-thousand-year timeline in his head, having coffee with me, his oldest grandchild, and perhaps, wishing for another flood. All of his grandchildren, plus himself, makes eight.

The wind whips up dirt from the vacant lots where even weeds won't grow. A truck sighs to a stop at the intersection outside the Burrito Inn where we met him after he went to Sunday School. This morning he skipped the church service because we are passing through town.

Earlier Gail and I had stopped at the old Comanche Spring. We looked through the chain links at the dry hole, the white casing lidded and locked, where an average of twenty-two million gallons of water a day used to flow before the richest man in the Trans-Pecos region drilled wells a few miles west of town and began pouring the water on cotton and alfalfa fields.

My grandfather says he raises burros because they are the biblical beasts of burden, carried Jesus into town, and now wear crosses on their backs. My mother says he raises burros for the agricultural tax exemption.

She is one of the faithful, one who never skips her yearly checkup or a dental appointment. Today the phone rings constantly, and she talks and talks and talks. She uses handy phrases, polishing them with each caller. Her laugh is high and brittle, cheerful and fragile.

Yesterday the doctor told us that she is a prime candidate for mastectomy, that she is a survivor. She asked God for the opportunity to grow to be more like Him. Now she wants to give the opportunity back, but she keeps saying *amen* into the phone. Holding nothing close and nothing sacred, she fills the air with words: medical oncologist, implantation of the port, stage one, grade three, pathology, malignant, invasive, lymph node mapping, hormone therapy. I haven't actually heard her say the word *cancer* yet.

She is one half of my genetic make-up, one of the twists in my spiral. She is the pieces of me that make me throw my hands up in despair, and yet, I fall in love with her all over again, not because I must, as an infant at her breast, but because she is by god worth it. She is my past, and I am watching my possible future. She has sensitive skin, and we both have chubby knees. She drinks coffee to stay warm on winter afternoons, decaf. After years of not watching television, she watches *Without a Trace* and *Murder She Wrote* and the Hallmark channel. She talks baby talk to her dogs, like she never would to her children or grandchildren. She irons the pillowcases and watches romantic movies, preferring the ones with no sex scenes or bad words. The candles in her home have white unlit wicks and a thin layer of dust on top of the wax. She gets tired of thinking up new things to cook for dinner. From her I inherit the genetic predisposition for osteoporosis, heart disease, skin cancer, Alzheimer's, and breast cancer. Genes that could keep me small and safe, careful and cautious, boring and banal, mundane and musty.

And what have I passed on to my children, Oscar and Lily?

At the hospital everyone comments on how much my sister Molly and I look like our mother. She sits up gaily after surgery, a cheerful hostess in a semi-private room until she pushes the button on the morphine pump and her inhibitions are masked by the drug. Then she says what she is thinking but would never say if it weren't for the fog. Molly plugs a curling iron in beside the IV stand and curls our mother's hair before visitors arrive, and Mom plucks the hospital gown away from her neck to peer down at the flat place on the left side of her chest.

Mom is retired from teaching seventh-grade English. She swims with the Aqua Babes three mornings a week. She reads to the preschoolers in the public library every Thursday and helps with chess club in the local elementary school twice a month. She rides the bus across an enormous university campus, marveling at how everyone stares at their iPhones, but she has learned to text so she can communicate with the young people she is caring for with Bible studies and home-cooked meals. She plays the piano while they sing. Every few months she polishes the silver she received at her wedding shower before she married my father. She orders blue-green algae, $40 for one hundred capsules, and liquid stevia drops from a health food website. She juices carrots, mangos, apples, celery, bell peppers, and parsley, drinking the brownorange soup like medicine. Anything to make the rapidly developing cells in her body go away. Together we read the ingredients on the tub of fake butter. When I mention chemicals in our environment, she glances at the pink packets of artificial sweetener beside the coffee pot. She threw out the Pine-Sol.

My youngest brother flew in from California for the mastectomy. We had a family reunion in the crowded hallway of the research hospital, and the nurses kept their faces neutral as they navigated around us. My grandfather watched the orderlies wheel his daughter out of surgery. He doesn't want to lose her the way he's already lost her mother.

Her healing is normal and progressive, but when I mention that I might go home on Thursday she gets tired and weak, has some pain around the drain site. When I tell her how happy I am that the new anti-emetic drug worked so well after surgery because it might also make chemotherapy less horrific, she says, "Well, I don't know. We'll see." Turns out, I was wrong, so very wrong.

I don't use the word *pray* anymore. It brings to mind corners and closets, cymbals and gongs. I tell my friends that I am sending good thoughts toward them when they are crying, but what I am more likely to do is recite Wendell Berry's poem "Peace of Wild Things" as often as I can, like a rosary without beads. A rosary with birds.

When my grandmother died, my grandfather spent hours tending her grave. Every day he drove to the site where caskets are sunk beneath the caliche soil, covered over with Bermuda grass. He took flowers and decorations. Pink and yellow tulips at Easter. A wreath at Christmas. Miniature American flags, yellow ribbons, plastic pumpkins, any excuse to visit where she lay. He went daily at first. Then weekly. And now, on her birthday, I ride along with him as he takes red roses wrapped in crinkly green paper. When she was alive he gave her flowers on holidays, and I don't even know if she liked them.

He hasn't been here all spring. We prop the vase against the hot June wind while he complains that the cemetery caretakers don't water the grass often enough. To me the grounds look better than most of West Texas as the drought continues. I thought losing her would kill him, but on his ninety-second birthday, he and a friend went to McDonald Observatory. They went to see the stars, the infinite heavens. After lunch at the fanciest place around, they sat down in the lobby and fell asleep, their heads leaned back on the comfortable couches.

On that same day, we were branding calves two states away and a B25 flew over our heads. Gail exclaimed about it being the plane my grandfather flew in World War II. The heat of the day left with the roar of the plane and I sat chilled. For some reason, I thought of those abandoned red roses beside my grandmother's headstone.

It is a scary thing, really. At first, the doctors determined that the mastectomy was enough; they got all the bad cells with surgery. No chemo or radiation necessary. But down the trail two years later we find out differently. Now it is time for the hard climb.

My father's eyes grow wet and his voice is unreliable when he hears us talking about wigs, scarves, buying yarn for crocheted caps, and sweeping the bathroom floor yet again, but, as the week drags on, I don't think it's the loss of her hair he is grieving. We start making minor bald jokes despite him. He speaks fluently of chemo cocktails, white blood cell count, bad days, dexamethasone, what time the cancer center opens, and which nurse will give the most direct answers. This is only her second treatment.

I cut off her hair the first afternoon I came to stay. I shaved her head with clippers the next afternoon while my father was away from the house on an errand. He tells me quietly that her personality is changing when she uses a peevish tone of voice to tell him that no she does *not* want him to read aloud to her and to *go away* and leave her alone because she feels bad. He reads the menu from the Chinese restaurant with free delivery for orders over $10, gazing into the take-away boxes I carry in, gauging how many meals he will be able to make out of two lunch entrées, $5.25 each, asking me how much he would have to tip the delivery person. He finally offers to shave his own head in solidarity, but laughs and says he was only joking anyway when she wryly turns him down.

He washes the car until it gleams, using Windex on the chrome wheels, and he looks at the calendar over and over because he knows the treatment will come around again.

I woke before dawn on my birthday to an olive flycatcher singing the same three notes 'round and 'round. There is heaven—and then there are these quiet moments. And I thought of gifts, listed them in the dawn:

A long-view photo I'll call *Where I Ride* and I'll send it to my father; a Gila monster; a black hawk that did not fly, but rather, talked us down the canyon.

A bear track; a lion track; the shell of a crawdad bleached white by the sun but blushing pink when I turn it over.

The turkey buzzard in his heraldic pose; a coyote trotting boldly up to drink right across the tank from us; two small does that followed shortly after in the almost dusk; plus the gift of the collared lizard standing in the top of a shoulder-high cedar tree stretching tall to grab the last few rays of day. The cow that touched my hand with her nose. The common things like egg shells beneath the swallows' nests; globe mallow blooming; and the big white horse standing at attention, looking at cows he sees before I do.

And, of course, the creek.

I drank the wild water.

We didn't eat pizza or watch a movie or go on a date. We didn't hear the new song on the radio, or get dressed up, or even have ice for our toddy that last night in camp. We smelled of sweat and wind. I hadn't seen a shower or cosmetics in five days. But we had T-bone steaks and squash cooked with butter and cheese—the last cool things from the cooler. The next morning, I made banana pancakes from soft, camp-weary fruit.

I found a dried red-capped toadstool for my shelf at home as well as a partial point. We drank a beer in the shade while the calves nursed hard at their mothers' bags, suckling relief after being mistreated by our hands. We saw a bullfight with dust and horns and adrenaline and testosterone and bellows. We rode on by.

I watched the sunrise the morning after my birthday. I saw, too, the sunset, after dragging back to headquarters with fatigue. A hummingbird drank from the water hose as I rescued my garden from the heat, fresh eggs bundled in the hem of my shirt, and I looked forward to that shower.

And I thought of the next birthday, but not for long.

San Angelo, Texas, June 2016

We do hopeful things like save avocado seeds, spearing them with toothpicks and resting their bottoms in jars of water. Hopeful because we expect to be here to refill the jar when the water evaporates below the seed. Hopeful because we are making future avocado trees.

My ninety-four-year-old grandfather laments aging in a way that makes me wonder where he's been all these years while his friends and family have been exiting planet Earth in waves. Sleeping in front of the television, volume high, is my best bet. He's from a generation that believes in capitalism and manifest destiny and that science is going to save us all. He is shocked and bewildered when the nurse explains that no, there is no cure for congestive heart failure. He's had it for fifteen years. He has seen the global population go from 1.9 billion to over 7 billion in his lifetime. When he sees someone on the television he asks where they are from. When the answer is somewhere foreign to his understanding like Romania or Nigeria he says, "Well, everyone has to live somewhere."

He shakes his head with regret that his grandchildren are having to read the horrible things in the newspaper. I am the oldest grandchild and I agree.

He sings to us with his now-quavery voice. We remember when it was strong. He sings hymns. He sings "Brown Eyes Crying in the Room" and I think maybe it is just a silly mistake as he recovers from a serious infection. But no, several days later he sings the same song, with the same mistaken lyrics. Maybe because my grandmother didn't have blue eyes. He demands that my sister and I sing with him, "America the Beautiful."

I am not accustomed to being in a home with a television, so I've put in earbuds to block the flow of propaganda, no longer laughing with my sister when an ad comes on for UNICEF, the SPCA, the American Indian Association, Publisher's Clearing House. He's given. To all of them. And now there is a balance owed of $234 to PCH. We told them he died. He has boxes of dish towels and piles of junk from various 501C3s. *Thank you for your support.* I got a pair of socks with wolves or coyotes howling at an orange moon from the pile.

I am reading a book by Jim Harrison, *Returning to Earth*, containing the sentence, "On another level he was very attractive in a rawboned way and I admit that I felt my bottom become warmer than the rest of my body." The oxygen machine sighs in and out and I glance up at my grandfather resting on the couch. He only wears the O2 when he's sleeping. When he is awake and complains of being short of breath, we put the pulse oximeter on his finger. He immediately feels better. He doesn't differentiate between the monitor and the machine. No way could my bottom feel at all warm in this situation, though I long for a connection to remind me that I am sensual and youngish and very much breathing. My O2 level stays at 98 percent most of the time. I haven't checked it when I am sleeping.

We are supposed to seek wisdom from our elders. So how do you make it to ninety-four, minus your prostate and with only half a heart in working order, years after your wife is gone and still eating like a field hand three meals a day? "Always make plans for next week." I take this to mean that we should make sure to have something to look forward to. I try not to flinch when he yells, "Hey!" at me from the couch. I tell him the day of the week four times over breakfast. Yes, one of the pills is a stool-softener.

When I finally return home, the avocado seeds are hard and dry, their bottoms six inches above the stagnant water in the jars. I wasn't here. I throw them away but still look hopeful toward next week.

Let's make guacamole. Barefoot.

Give me a sky burial so I might finally fly.

Give me a pine box so that as it collapses back into the earth, my bones will join the duff with the helpful worms.

My veins reject embalming fluid and my skin pales to consider spackle or a viewing with open casket and the perfume of hothouse blooms, the gentle murmur of family in black.

Don't send flowers, the ovaries of plants chopped off and wrapped up, paid for with a credit card. Take instead some of my ashes to fertilize your rose bushes or, better yet, the spinach and summer squash. The blossoms will be early morning coffeehouses for the bees.

Give me a sky burial. Whoever arrives first gets the best parts.

Carrizozo, New Mexico, and someone's car alarm is going off. That's the way a song begins. I have no way of knowing how the story ends, so I write my way through it with ink on the page. I know how some stories end. They end with death rattles and *in lieu of flowers* . . .

We've laid you to rest, Rusty McCall, and I believe you were ready to rest. You were only twenty-eight years old, and I miss you. I tell people that your mother is my best friend, but for almost five years, *you* were my best friend. When I would sit down at my computer in the mornings, it was you who greeted me. The chat screen would light up with your good morning, your questions about how my day was going. You talked to me in text when deafness robbed you of so many things. While your speech could still be understood, you talked to Gail on the telephone using the Cap-Tel system. He had to be careful about cussing, afraid to offend the silent and invisible transcriptionist who typed his words on the screen for you to read. Even that method of communicating eventually became too hard.

Your ripple touched so many.

What is closure? This weekend, people gathered on your mountain. Your mother arranged your saddle and gun and photos of you as a small boy for us all to see. During the service, Gail's guitar was out of tune for that second song, a fact that you would not have been able to appreciate since your hearing left you long before you left us, but still, you would have grinned, your perfect lopsided grin, if I had written it down for you.

So many people showed up to wish you farewell. It is a long drive up your mountain, but still they came, your blood family plus your extended one, the cowboy poetry and music family, part of your world since you were the smallest one at the microphone, saying your poems. Jean was late, missed the whole service. But later, after we had eaten too much food, she sang all her funny songs. And Brooksie brought her new puppy. Later, even your nieces recited poems in the round-robin night.

Carrizozo, New Mexico, on our way home, and the car alarm is silenced, though I don't know how or why. I am headed back west, and tomorrow I'll kindle a new fire, roll out my bed, and my story goes on.

Sometimes a prayer looks like sitting in silence . . . with a broken heart.

The forest is messy. The trees do not grow in rows, and some of them grow in a tangle. The vines are rude, and the wildflowers take over the open spaces. Some people call them weeds. The trees that are dying have no respect for those that are fresh and pale green, and there are no neat boundaries to separate the old from the young, the young from the old. Toadstools spring up in the woodchip piles of decaying logs. Low-growing vegetation begs the ancient ones for the sunlight filtering through the canopy. Tree roots make mounds to be stepped over, and chiggers and snakes lurk in the high grass. In the forest, there is no careful delineation between life and death.

Moonshine and Namaste

Our January sun this year feels like April. My hens have already begun laying, a truncated holiday for the complicated systems inside these simple animals. October, November, and December were full-up squares with multi-colored ink in layers—a scoop of duty and obligation to go with celebration—add a business or doctor appointment beside a thrill or some sushi. Those three months burst their seams into the new year, spilled over onto ten or twelve days.

And then stopped. Becalmed, I float. I choose which pool—sleepy-headed rest and relief, a true winter's pool of Demeter's keening loss, or the rolls and chops of creative energy.

But mainly I do chores, gentle chores, moving smoothly from one to another, all in this warmer January sunshine. I feed animals and fold clothes and write down poems as I skim them from the tops of coffee cups. I remove balls of dust from beneath furniture and cut up celery for soup. I stoke the fire after the early dark. I gather eggs.

Three days ago, I found myself in a sheltered corner of an office complex in conversation with a man who knows what it is to be becalmed. He speaks of freefall. His wife recently died of breast cancer she refused to treat with traditional medicine. The tumor erupted from beneath the skin in spite of herbs, meditation, and the power of positive thinking. There was no stopping this thing with diet or juicing or sleep. He has emerged from the cave of pain and helplessness and emergency rooms and hospice into this January sun. Into freefall. He doesn't have to be anywhere or do anything. His gestures remind me of a swimmer's.

"What if none of this matters?" He beams at me. Am I listening? "What if we are all just moonshine?"

I drive home. Moonshine. My always-happy-with-words brain offers me two definitions and I am content with both. I can feel them both as they slide down into my belly.

I grew up with Mother's heels clicking on the hard floors of Sunday mornings. The smell of roast and potatoes in the oven. A grouchy scurry in uncomfortable clothes to the car, no peace on this day, Lord's Day. I've sat in many pews, taken notes on many sermons, sung many hymns that are now completely part of my DNA. I do everything I can to get out of weddings or funerals if they are held in a Christian house of worship.

Two years ago, Gail was asked to bring some of his songs and the poems he recites to a congregation that focuses on spiritual living and enlightenment with no foundation in any particular faith. Now he is on their regular rotation as a soloist during their Sunday morning service. We go every two months or so. The first time, I resisted. Feeling like a guilty schoolgirl cutting class, I ran our errands during his sound check and the 10:00 a.m. meditation, sliding into my chair (no pews here) just as the service began. Gail leaned over to whisper, "The meditation was nice." The next time we went, I tried it. Now I own a purple meditation cushion.

I still get anxious and irritable at the sound of my own heels clicking around on Sunday mornings. I'd rather smell roasting beef on a Thursday afternoon. But I love to sing, and even in this strange worship service where they light a candle for each of the major world religions (yes, even for me when they get to the one for the earth-based faiths) they sing songs I have heard all my life. My body and soul resist every time we are asked to stand and sing, every time some enthusiast begins to clap, every time some smiling sweet old lady reaches for my hand at the end of service, but I sing, even the positively-altered lyrics:

Yes, there is peace on earth
And yes it begins with me.

Namaste and moonshine.

Bat Flight

A mouse—a mouse with wings to take her places. A mouse with sonar and appetite. A mouse with reputation, mystery, mythology. She is the size of a man's thumb, but rounder, fatter, softer. Her right-side-up is most of the world's up-side-down. She hangs with minute, fragile grip from the rough rock of the cavern ceiling. She hangs in the concentrated smother of her colony, one of the masses, one of the brown threads of the carpet spread on the ceiling of the cave.

Through the long day, she sleeps against the pull of gravity. Through the long day, she waits for the night. Through the long day, her hunger builds until the time when she will wing her way over the desert to feast, flying away from the warm, safe cave, a creature of instinct, navigating the night sky.

A mouse that flies.

She has no window to the west to tell her that it is sundown, but when the time is right, with no drama, no indecision, no hesitation, no doubt, she loosens her grip and drops in a momentary concession to the direction of the earth's core; she says yes to its pull. She unfolds her wings, breathes the damp air through flaring nostrils, and arrests her fall to soar out into the entrance cave to begin circling, preparing to leave through the natural mouth of the cavern into the sky.

With a hundred-dollar bill in the sole of his boot, my father went to Idaho the summer he was sixteen. He had started out working as a roustabout in the Permian Basin oilfields, but when he heard that Johnny Hardaway was going north to see new country, he decided to go along. The youngest of my grandparents' five children, he weighed 110 pounds with his boots, hat, belt, and wire-rimmed glasses on and looked much younger than sixteen. His father simply handed him the hundred-dollar bill and told him not to spend it unless he needed a bus ticket home.

Once in Idaho, the boys bucked bales of hay at a dairy, and that first night, he and Johnny rolled their blankets out inside the dairy barn. When they woke the next morning, their faces were solid black from the specks that fell from a ceiling carpeted with flies. From then on, they slept outside under the night sky.

Johnny finally got them a job on a ranch, but the rancher wouldn't let my dad go up into the mountain meadows with the older hands. He had to stay down at headquarters and drive the hay rake. When everyone else went into town to celebrate the 4th of July, he had to stay behind to do chores. He had never milked cows before and didn't know how to use the chain hobbles that the rancher left hanging on a hook beside the stall. The rancher came home and scratched his head at the rope burns on his cows' ankles. Those Texas boys.

Dad and Johnny frequented Kitty's Hot Hole that summer, an establishment where a quarter bought a longneck bottle of beer. For another quarter, the cowboys could soak in the hot spring, towel and soap included. Kitty's had wooden floors spread with salt and sawdust and a jukebox that played music for free. They danced.

It was in Kitty's where Dad met a man who claimed to be a rawhide braider. He took the boys out beside the bar to a 1940 Ford Coupe parked under the trees. He showed them his wares of detailed and intricate craftsmanship. Dad bought reins and *romal*, the most beautiful he had ever seen. Back inside, the bartender told him that the man did not do all of that work himself, but instead had married a "squaw" who stayed home and worked the rawhide while her husband travelled over the road, peddling her wares.

Dad caught a ride back to Texas with Johnny's parents right before school started in the fall. On the way home he bought a Navajo blanket, 100 percent wool—black, brown, gray, and white. The hundred-dollar bill was still in his boot.

In May 2006, I drove away from home in a gold car with my daughter Lily beside me and too many clothes in my duffle bag. We took a fifteen-dollar tent, a single-burner camp stove, and not enough blankets. We were gone seven weeks. I brought home a jar of water from Crazy Woman Creek, a navy-blue sarong from Springdale, Utah, a book of poetry, and a pottery coffee mug. We left again in 2007 when my husband got fired from his job in the Texas Panhandle. This time we were loaded down, the whole family off to an adventure in California, seasonal work, a romantic name for being homeless as soon as the summer of packing mules and tending guests was over. I left again, left my husband that time, later that year. I took nothing. And I arrived here on the Spider in 2008 with very little other than an unpublished manuscript, a handmade saddle, boxes of books and a love for wood smoke.

A misunderstood symbol of darkness and evil, of blood loss and disease, painted black and given fangs even in caricature. A bat caught in your hair is the stuff of nightmares.

The bat is a winged mammal. Babies are born in the late spring and cluster in the nursery drinking one third of the mother's body weight in milk each day. During the night, the mothers stay close to the cave, returning often to feed their young. At the end of six weeks, the infants join the mothers in their nightly exodus. They learn to fly.

I went to Carlsbad Caverns several times as a child and teenager, but my father never let us stay long enough to see the evening bat flight. On our camping trip, Lily and I sat in dry desert air on hard stone benches for over an hour listening to the rangers discuss the Brazilian free-tailed bat and the habits that cause them to fly off into the desert each evening. They spoke in vague terms saying "usually" and "most of the time" and "when the weather is good." There is no button to be pushed, no wire to be tripped that will make this natural phenomenon happen.

The bats fly when the bats fly.

They don't fight the dance they do for survival and because they must.

They don't reason it out each day.

They don't use logic or science or a spreadsheet.

Instinct bids them leave the cave each evening and fly toward the rivers where the moths and mosquitoes become a meal to sustain them when they return to hang sleeping while tourists marvel at their bedchamber décor each day.

When she's circled long enough or when the disk of sky seen through the mouth of the cave is the right hue, she dips through the opening, swirling with the rest, just one in a spiraling mass of clichéd black shapes, drifting like a plume of smoke out of a flameless hole in the ground, a signal that the night has begun. The stream of bats floats northward before it curves back to the east, becoming a trickle as each individual breaks away to hunt in solitude through the night, droplets of water independent of the stream.

I learned to camp, almost too well. I learned about the blue flame of camp stoves, about leaving, about packing up and moving, and about wedding rings that go off and on.

Sometimes journeys wake us up. Sometimes we fly. Sometimes we go back to sleep until the snooze alarm rings.

One night, at Benson Lake deep in Yosemite National Park, my body aching from riding a horse all day, lifting and shoveling and cooking all evening, my brain exhausted from being the one in charge, I lay in my bedroll sans tent, burrowed down into the sand, and realized that the dark shapes above me, darting between the pines, eating insects from above the lake and its broad shore, were bats.

I knew the dark by then, too. I knew how to cover up my watch and my cell phone face and simply be.

To be in our hay barn here on the Spider at 3:00 a.m. from May through October is to stand in a cloud of bats, to stand in their swirl, to be overwhelmed by the sound of their wings and their voices. Gail says he's only been bumped a few times as he ducked through the cloud to get hay for horses and early morning rides, but one morning a bat landed on the front of my denim shirt. We both, the bat and I, sat very still until she flew away.

Five species of bats live here during the warm months. We have the Brazilian free-tailed, *Tadarida brasiliensis*, the western yellow bat, *Lasiurus xanthinus*, the pallid bat, *Antrozous pallidus*, Townsend's big-eared, *Plecotus townsendii* and the smallest bat in the United States, the western pipistrelle, *Pipistrellus hesperus*. There could be others, but they are difficult to get a good look at as they dance through the gloom—probably several types of myotis, very common bats. The hoary bat, *Lasiurus cinereus*, the largest in the United States, also lives on the ranch, but he is a solitary rooster. He doesn't live in the barn but in the riparian bottoms of deep desert canyons. I have only seen him once. Miles and miles from any pavement, horseback, I saw him hanging from the limb of a juniper tree, his long soft fur frosted, hoary, different.

Don't Talk to Strangers

May 2006

In the steadily deepening dark, I can't see the moss and silty mud that rises in a cloud around me every time I move in the hot water. I know from earlier in the evening that as soon as the water stops stirring, it clears, the particles settling back to coat the sandy bottom and my skin that is slowly reddening with heat in the hand-dug, rock-lined soaking pool. As the night air cools, bluish steam begins to rise from the black surface of the water. Amber solar lights glow along the edges of the pools using the energy they stored through the bright afternoon. The sound of rushing, falling water never ceases, coming both from the river on two sides of the campground and the spring flowing down into the pool where I sit with my arms wrapped around my knees. I can see our tent from here, softly glowing with lantern light as Lily reads her book, safely cocooned for the night.

When I decided to come on this trip, I wrote what was for me a rather terse e-mail to my family and friends, explaining where I would be for so many weeks as well as asking for reading recommendations. I wanted to fill a box with books I had never read before. I received many replies from the friends of my heart—encouraging, celebratory, envious, offering suggestions of places I shouldn't miss along the way, and, of course, a phenomenal reading list. Some of them even sent me books in the mail as bon voyage gifts. From my friends of circumstance and chance, I got a few replies, most of them full of incredulity, horror, and warnings, explaining why such a journey did not at all appeal to them personally, asking questions like, "Where will you plug in your hair dryer?" and "What about the bears?" From my immediate family, I received only one reply, one line, and it came from my mother. *Be careful, and don't talk to strangers.*

When Al walks up, I sit still in the water. His hair is wild and blended with his beard. His clothes are wrinkled and worn. His eyes are cautious, never fully present. I don't think he notices me at first, or maybe he is waiting for a sign of acceptance. Lily and I have our own bag of dirty, camp-stained, duffle-bag wrinkled clothes in the car. My own unwashed hair is tied firmly under an orange bandanna. I know from my born place what it feels like not to know where I fit.

I had hesitated to move our tent from the free, semi-developed Upper Scorpion Campground at the base of the Gila Cliff Dwellings to this $4-a-night even more primitive site here at the hot spring. But the strange, twisting sculptures of desert driftwood, metal, and glass guarding the soaking pools, standing bravely in danger of washing away if the river floods, lured us in spite of the grandmotherly warning from the Forest Service volunteer who leaned across the visitors' center desk to hiss that the privately owned campground was "clothing optional."

Al strips off his clothes and eases into the large pool, moaning aloud at the heat and lying back to rest on a large rock. His relishing of the hot water soothes away my inhibitions and soon we are discussing Salinger, Steinbeck, Stegner, Joan Baez, Dylan, and Kerouac. I learn that it has taken Al two days to thumb a ride forty-four miles from Silver City up into the wilderness. When I ask him where he is from, he replies simply, "I wintered in Yuma."

As it grows completely dark around us, he tells me of his time in Austin, Texas, of the bars and the music. He tells me that he avoids Tucson due to a misunderstanding involving whisky and court dates. He lifts himself out of the water to sit steaming on a rock beside the pool, totally nude, totally human, his back sculpted, his arms lean and aging, his legs thin and male. He tells me about the hamburger some "rich dudes up here to go fishing" bought him earlier in the day in a restaurant that "even served wine." He talks about what a relief it is to leave the towns and cities behind, to be here in this place of wild animals, river water, and privacy.

"The stinkin' cities make me feel like we are all fish in one of them big tanks. You know, aquariums?" His eyes beg me to get it, to really listen, to understand. "It's just that someone forgot to clean it."

He ducks his head. The second time in the evening that he tells the same story, pausing in the same place, I realize that he has been reciting it like a poem to himself all day, rehearsing it as he held his thumb out to each climbing, laboring tourist's vehicle.

"The fuckers are slowly poisoning us all . . . our bodies with fumes and noise, our minds with violence and politics. The fuckers."

Twice in the course of the evening, Jim, the caretaker of the campground, walks over to the pool, supposedly to check on the temperature and make small talk, but truly, I know, to check on me, to make sure the vagrant isn't bothering me. He is taking care of me as men in my life have always taken care of me.

Al borrows some lotion, pumping it from the big bottle I bought in Silver City. He tells me his name. I write down the title of a book by Kerouac that he recommends, trying not to drip on the pages of my notebook. He wonders aloud where to obtain fresh drinking water, and then, with no fanfare or farewell, he dresses and wanders away from the pool, off to sleep at his designated campsite, tentless, dug into the sand for warmth.

With Al gone and Jim retired for the night, I am alone at the pool. I stand up from the steaming water. The high-desert mountain air immediately chills my skin. I cross my arms, grab the hem of my streaming T-shirt, and strip it off over my head. I toss it into a soggy heap on a rock, pull off my clinging shorts, and lower myself back down into the hot water.

Clothing optional.

She'll Do to Float the River With

~for Lily

Water, in order to nourish, must be pumped up out of the ground, caught as it falls from the sky, desalinated if it comes from the oceans, harnessed, heated, contained, stored, hoarded. Only the water dwelling between the sky and the dirt is presently useful. That in the depths or temporarily hanging as mist above the earth is out of easy reach.

Running water takes the simplest path, the path with the most downward flow, the path in the direction of the center of the earth. In its conflicts, it moves to either side or carries that which impedes it along on its way. Moving water is never mournful or unable to do its job. It is cheerful and capable, nourishing and causing all to flourish and change, sometimes destructive and uncaring. Water can be wasted, contaminated, studied. But it can never be destroyed.

When I was a child, we didn't take many vacations. I do remember, though, my father and mother telling us to "load up!" and then driving north along Highway 54 until they got tired of us fighting or fidgeting. My father would pick a likely spot, pull over and say, "You moguls hike to the top of that mountain!" We would clamber out, duck between the strands of barbed wire, and look up at the steep, rocky hill in front of us.

We thought he made up the word *mogul* just for us. We also thought any hill was a mountain.

Mom and Dad would sit in the truck with the windows rolled down and talk in peace. The only rules were that we watch for snakes and come back to the truck when we heard the horn honking.

The beauty of parenthood is that sometimes, in order to be a good parent, one must do something just for fun. My life is better because Lily taught me to play and to dream, and one year she gave up a summer at the county swimming pool to go hiking and camping with her crazy mother.

I learned to stop for ice cream cones and listen to audio books about dragons.

I floated one piece of the Virgin River in an inner tube three times in one day.

Getting into the river is awkward, the vehicle cumbersome. We carry our tubes across the street, accidentally dragging them on the dirt or sidewalk, and through an RV park to the sandy bank where the wide, flat, shallow river looks used. The bite of the cold water makes it something to be avoided rather than embraced or trusted or floated upon. We clamber gracelessly aboard the rubber tubes with their canvas covers, and the seat of my swimsuit is immediately soaked, wicking the cold water further up my torso. Our bodies weigh the tubes down, ground them, plant them on the sandy bottom. With arms and legs awkwardly sticking out over the sides and heads tilted stiffly forward, we rock back and forth, paddle with strangely bent limbs, barely reaching the water, hoping to push our inflated vehicles out into the center where the river will take over and make the journey graceful.

We don't trust the river, but instead expend our energy to help it.

The river will always carry us downstream, never upstream. It might move more slowly than we'd like. It might, at times, move more swiftly, bashing us against the rocks and separating me from my daughter. It might run us aground amidst the shallows of a big curve, but the river always moves on.

Here at the beginning we wiggle and paddle and wonder what is going to happen and squeal when drops of icy water hit our sun-warmed skin. We shift around in our tubes, seeking a more comfortable position than nestled with arms and legs flung over the sides and neck propped up from behind. We seem to move too slowly to be going anywhere.

The man who rented us our tubes in Springdale, Utah, and showed us on the map how the Virgin River runs through the town, also explained that *dilution is the solution*. Ammonia and other chemicals washed out of the river of our bloodstreams should be released into the water to be absorbed and carried away by the snowmelt as it flows over rocks and sand and tree roots, as it widens and calms, as it narrows and splashes.

There is that moment, that private moment, when one must fight the conditioning of society and sit in the heat released from the body, sit uncomfortably in what is most certainly ours, acknowledge that we are human and that we must release what needs to be released, no matter how unpleasant. The river is faithful to carry it away.

Lily's father and I said "I love you" during the first week after we met. We were so young, and he was so much fun. We began to speak of *when* rather than *if* we got married. We didn't court. We simply were. Sixteen years later, the *I love yous* were in the thousands and the kisses were in the millions and the realities of *us* outnumbered the details of who we were before. And who were we now? Neither one of us was quite sure. When I left Texas on this crazy and unnecessary journey, we were on a seven- to ten-day cycle of fighting and silence. We were sitting in a pool of who we had become.

The intensity of love is diluted by days and days and nights, meals eaten, boundaries crossed, words said, encounters in the dark, sunrises, sunsets, bills paid, boxes packed and unpacked, arguments that dissolve into thin air when we get out of the pickup, crises handled, children birthed or lost. On this seven-week journey, seven weeks to sleep in a tent and hike the trails and float this river, I wondered if *we* would endure the whims of *me*. The trip suddenly seemed necessary.

There is no geometry to the river, no perfect angles, no straight lines. The only absolute proof in the river is that it flows downhill. Close to the bank, under the willows, it often goes in whirlpool circles or slows into shallow, stagnant pools of muddy tadpoles.

The river's pace is dictated by the terrain, and we can't see what is coming around the bend. Sometimes the bend leads us to half a mile of rapidly flowing, rocky water and there is no time to prepare, no time to marshal our forces, no time to grasp hands and vow to stay together. Once through the rapids, I wipe the water from my eyes and face, look around to see if my daughter is still in her tube. It takes a while for my heartbeat to slow down.

Butt up! is the rule for the rapids. We laughed at the man in dreadlocks who warned us about this as we chose our tubes, but after the first narrow fling through a small series of rapids, I look over at Lily to see tears running down her face. That night, in the tent, I see a long narrow bruise on her thin little back. My own hip aches. Neither one of us will forget again to arch our backs and brace with our elbows, getting our vulnerable parts up, away from the hidden rocks that bash our bones. What kind of mother am I?

The second time we float this portion of river, another group leaves just ahead of us from the RV park. As we pass them in mid-float, I see an overweight boy of twelve or thirteen, standing in the shallows of the bend, yelling at his mother who is floating along with three younger children.

He hates this. The water is too cold. The rocks are too hard. He was going too fast. He has run aground. The water moves too slowly. Next time he is staying in the hotel room—an enclosed, narrow, careful coffin where there are no rocks, no icy snowmelt, no need to pee inside your swimsuit, no rapids that fling you along beyond your control, no muddy banks, no hummingbirds. Just a prescribed, programmed feed coming out of a box. Insulation from the pain, the discomfort, the wonder.

I am the right kind of mother. Today.

Drenched by the rapids back behind us, we float along on the very surface of a deep, broad, slow-moving swimming hole lined on either bank with willows and elderly trees that graciously host hammocks and rope swings. Lawns rise in manicured folds on either side, leading up to old houses with fresh paint.

The river turns dark here, darker still up close to the muddy undercut banks. I lie my head back on the tube, holding on to this moment of peace, rest, and the warm sun drying my T-shirt.

The sound of the rapids is fading and the rush of the next foaming water has not yet reached my ears when I hear a new sound. The whirring and buzzing of wings in the air. I open my eyes and see, looking me right in the eye, a brilliant hummingbird, come to say hello, come to offer a moment of magic before changing course with an imperceptible shift to dip into the water and drink. Beside me, Lily is smiling and holding her breath.

There were no notices or trumpets. No signs saying, "Posted: Hummingbirds ahead." If we hurry or we sleep or we complain and whine about last week's bruises, we miss their presence, miss their greeting, miss their brilliant wings. If we are busy paddling, trying to leave the long, slow, boring parts, we won't notice their minute and fragile existence. There is no law demanding that magic moments stay. They may leave at any time. And do.

The hummingbirds are free of the river, but we move within its flow.

When this trip ends, we will go home to the Texas Panhandle and try to explain the things we've seen. The public lands we've slept on, hiked on, floated on, explored. I'll go back, for a time, to a husband who is fun and willing and bigger than life. We've both been bruised by my bashing myself against the rocks of discontent and autonomy. But we've also both sat in wonder as life flows around the bends.

Lily will do to float the river with. She'll be quiet during the hummingbird moments, squeal with me in the rapids, laugh when the cold water washes up over our heads, compare bruises with me in the tent at night. She's willing to clamber out of the tube and push off from the rocks when we run aground and not worry about our clumsiness. More importantly, she will crawl out of the river at the landing, trudge up the sandy slope toward the shuttle waiting to take us back to the beginning, and turn to say through blue lips, "Wanna go again?"

She reminds me of her father.

Not Enough Snoopy Band-Aids

~for Oscar

When he was seventeen, he lived two states away. Homeschooled and ruined from the start by a mother who wears a Rolling Stones T-shirt, he chose to make his own way and shun the paths hacked into time by those who have gone before. He taught himself the old ways with leather and rawhide and horsehair and animals. He lived in the bunkhouse and rode the rough string. His job came with housing, as well as utilities, beef, health insurance, a company pickup, a steady paycheck, and that ain't too damned bad in the current economic atmosphere.

He was reluctant for me to take him out to eat, and I couldn't figure out why until we drove back up to his little house laden with the remains of our seafood Portofino, and he showed me the grill he welded for himself out of scrap metal. I ate again in a few hours, the beef he cooked for me over mesquite coals.

His alarm went off on Sunday mornings at the same time it went off on workdays, and he would get up to clean his little house, sweeping every week, mopping every other. I noticed he just cleaned around the piles of books stacked on the floor by the walls as music of all sorts blasted from the cd player. He watched MTV while he drank coffee in the mornings but told me that other than that he didn't watch much television. He tried to not watch any for a month but it cost him $300 at Barnes and Noble.

He called to ask me about sourdough starter and where he could find a non-electric coffee pot (no they don't sell them at Wal-Mart, go to the antique/junk store), and I promised to send him a box of books from my shelves. He sighed over the fact that he was born one hundred years too late.

Dear Son,

I will never be a good horsewoman. I will always be barely adequate in that department. And that is how I feel about being the mother of a grown son . . . as if I will never quite get the hang of it.

When you come into this house, you take up all the air. When we flew to Texas for your sister's graduation, you were the only person in the airport. When I watched you ride that bronc, tall and straight, I could feel where you grew up under my heart. You make me laugh harder than anyone I know.

When you were a small boy, you rushed headlong into owies. You would come crying, and I would get out the Mercurochrome (we called it Monkey's Blood) and the Snoopy Band-Aids, and I would make it all better, especially with a grape popsicle from the freezer.

It is not that easy any more. . . .

I am so glad I got up from the dinner table to answer my phone last night, but I would buy every popsicle in the world if I thought they might soothe the hurt from your voice. I have heard it several times in the last few years and it is never any easier for me to take . . . and the hard part is that I know I will hear it again.

Like your sister said, "That boy bruises easily." And you do. I wouldn't have it any other way, but oh, my son . . . my beautiful, smart, funny son . . . I don't have the right words to make these bruises go away.

See, you called to tell me that a friend has lost a child and that you didn't know how old the baby was but he was walking and saying things. I could hear the confusion in your voice . . . how could someone your age have a son when he should still be a son and a grandson himself?

And how will he go on living after that baby died?

You say, "Mom, that would be it for me. It would be over for me." And I want to scream at you that no, you would be strong enough, but I can't scream something that might be a lie . . . for you and for me both.

Go on breathing, kid, because I have to breathe, too.

I bought a tiny onesie that says, "Cool like my Dad." I should have bought it in a bigger size. You are a father now. And life is tough. And money is scarce. And you work harder than anyone I've ever known. And he's beautiful, that boy. And you were meant to be his dad. You will ruin him perfectly. Just as I ruined you.

Pretty

The butterfly rests gracefully in the cocoon. Her wings are colored and striped without her choosing.

The toad beneath the soil waits until it rains but does not choose whether her tadpoles grow legs or antlers.

They are becoming, always, and the metaphor works . . . up to a point.

We are becoming, too, but the difference is that we get to choose, choose what brilliant feathers we wear, what hot winds we blow, what weather boils inside our own soul.

We choose what diverging paths we take or whether we hike off cross-country to the beat of a new rhythm in our heads.

We are free to decide, free to move about the country, the planet, free to become the incredible or the mundane, the shining or the shadow. We are the ones who show up ready to receive our own bright rewards, our own clear sight when the shells and scales fall away.

Fifty-two butterflies, mashed flat under glass, held tightly in time to cotton batting. To open the frame would be to destroy the collection forever. To destroy them *further*, forever. All those feathered wings would crumble in the air.

The largest, in the center, is the size of my two palms, hinged together at my pulse points. Each wing holds the mystery of faceted light, and even the browns are translucent. The smallest two, transparent lacewings, are the width of my thumb. They are turned sideways, accent pieces along with the green scarab beetles dotted among the batting like buttons on a fancy couch. The butterflies' wings change color. The yellows love the nighttime lamplight, and the whites become lavender in the day. Royally purple.

This collection came from Brazil in the 1940s. All fifty-two brilliant fliers were netted, put to sleep, put to death, softened, arranged, pinned, sealed up expertly by a company now famous in antique circles for ashtrays and serving trays decorated with layers of insect wings in patterns, perhaps remnants, the leftover body parts of imperfect specimens, the uncollectable.

The identifying information for each butterfly is typed on company letterhead and glued to the back of the frame . . . genus, species, and gender, though only a few are female. The stationery has browned and crisped with age. The company, Zitrin Irmãos, spoke German, French, and English for the convenience of its customers, if not the butterflies. Some of them are actually moths. *Urania leilus. Morpho anaxibia. Anaea porphyrio. On parle français.*

In my imagination I become one of those peasants whose job was to wander the jungle, catching butterflies. I would have walked through the tangle silently, through the dripping rainforest being oh, so careful with my net. Would I have ceased to view them with awe? Would I have ceased to mourn a broken wing or a thorax oozing messy gel? Earning blood money.

They were worms once, caterpillars, inching their way through leaves, seeking fullness and darkness, spinning a place to dwell, a safe place of rebirth, expansion, transformation. They had to die to become, or at least sleep deeply. Sleeping to become beauty. They had the privilege of undergoing metamorphosis, coming out more fragile than they went in, but coming out more.

Anartia amathea is also called the scarlet peacock but the specimen in this collection has faded with time, the red now more orange. Whole legends are woven around the black witch, *Erebus odora*, from South America. *Catopsilia trite* hasn't faded a bit, is still a bright cheerful yellow. Pretty.

As I go through the year, learning more about each specimen, a new one each week, I exclaim over and over at the details, the patterns, the most nondescript moths becoming works of art when I get closer, see the waves of color that change as the day ages. They've been catching the light for longer than I've been alive. Two of them are now extinct, or so the Smithsonian website tells me. Each one could be the definition of beauty.

The butterflies cannot be in direct sunlight, for at the edges of the frame are the beginnings of decay that bright light will only exacerbate. In my office I place them where I can see them but they are shielded from the sun.

Before, I traveled light. Now I am glad to have this rare treasure, this antique that someone accidentally sold in an estate sale, this once-upon-a-time gift shipped home from a long-ago vacation, this belated Christmas gift that Gail forgot to give me until the first week in the new year. He knew I would love it. The heavy frame will be part of my life forever.

I still have the first dress I ever wore. It is framed, preserved under glass, along with the letter my Granny wrote to me when I was one week old explaining that she made it over a doll's pattern. She asked me to grow a little before she made the next one. I was born six weeks before my mother was ready. Granny tucked the dress and letter into a standard letter-sized envelope in 1970.

When I was ten years old my mother bought some aqua and white gingham and sewed a sundress that hung straight from my shoulders in a slight A-line, like a tent. I loved it because it left my whole body free. It became my uniform that summer, just white cotton panties and that simple dress that didn't touch me or bind me. Sometimes, when she thought of it, my mother made me wear shorts under it for modesty.

My mother made many of the garments my sister and I wore, and mid-summer was an orgy of sewing machine whir and the snick of shears on the Ethan Allen dining room table. I can still hear the rumble of those scissors as they sliced through the fabric atop the heavy, dark wood. She would call us away from our books and our play to be measured or to try on some garment-in-progress. We stood absolutely still to avoid pin pricks.

The fabric store in our little town was in one end of the funeral parlor. The lady who owned it was married to the undertaker. She set up her shop in the west corner of the building and the summer sun heated the room through the sliding glass doors in spite of heavy, insulated drapes. The shop was full of fabric and notions, rick-rack and spools of thread arranged in rainbows, and huge books of patterns. If you told her the right number, she could pull the paper pattern in its envelope out of a heavy metal drawer. It was magical at first and then boring and then frightening if all of a sudden we had to pee. And of course we had to pee . . . which meant we had to walk through the opposite door into the strangely cold funeral home, through the parlor, and down the hallway to the ladies' room. I never could decide if it was scarier when the parlor was dark and quiet or when it was lit up and adorned with wreaths and a casket.

Always, after our school clothes were sewn and fitted, I liked the fabric my sister chose better than mine.

My mother has naturally curly hair. She spent my childhood evenings wrapping my naturally straight hair on pink sponge rollers so that it wouldn't just "hang there, long and stringy" when I went to school or church the next day. My mother's rule was that if and when we began to faithfully (as in every day, morning and night) use the whole Mary Kay skin care regimen ($100 in 1985), then she would buy us the Mary Kay beauty products. Today I use coconut oil on my face morning and night, and sometimes forget to put on mascara when I go to town.

The year I was sixteen, we couldn't find a decent swimsuit in the JCPenny catalog. Decent meant one that wouldn't show I had actual breasts and wasn't cut too high on the legs. Finally, Mom bought heavy aqua knit and made me a swimsuit using the stretch stitch. Her sewing machine and bits of bright aqua littered the dining room. I wore one of my father's white Hanes undershirts over the finished suit, both in and out of the water.

Today, my favorite piece of cowboy gear is my chaps. My son, Oscar, spent hours making them for me, sewing and stamping and fitting them to my legs. He chose the conchos and a buckle with tiny rubies in it. They've been bloodied and scarred, but I feel like a queen as the long fringe sways and flaps around my ankles. They fit like my skin.

My favorite photograph of my daughter, Lily, was taken at Crazy Woman Creek in the Big Horn Mountains of Wyoming. In the photo she is ten years old, barefoot, a bandanna tied over her hair. She is wearing a simple sundress that hangs straight from her shoulders, not touching her or binding her. She is carrying a bucket of water to our campsite.

The photos of my mother when she was a young woman show her in slim-waisted dresses atop crinolines with a tall, ratted beehive of hair, white gloves, a corsage, and her own mother firmly behind the camera.

At the beginning of my teenage years, my mother told me she regretted ever shaving her legs. The hair on my legs was long and silky and translucent blond. But, a typical adolescent girl, I ended up in my best friend's bathroom, the door firmly locked against her mother and our younger sisters. I perched on the vanity with my feet in the sink while Sarah sat on the edge of the tub. I pulled the blade up my leg, gathering hair and soap suds as I went, and then, thrilled at the smooth path left behind, I moved the razor down to my ankle to make another pass. Sarah yelled at me, "Wait! Rinse it first! Don't you know anything?" She was a leg-shaving veteran of two weeks. I hear her scornful voice in my head every time I shave.

My razor is trendy and pink. It rests on the edge of the bathtub. The disposable cartridges come in many flavors . . . aloe with vitamin E, pomegranate extract, soothing moisture with milk and honey, shea butter and oatmeal. Fourteen dollars for a pack of three. I haven't used it in six months.

The hair on my legs and under my arms is long and silky and pretty. The world did not come to an end when I stopped shaving. But . . . it is not sundress season yet. It takes some courage to live our ideals and not all of them are worth living.

A woman is rarely told that her natural body smells good, with no potions or perfumes to cover up the real scent that lingers between her folds. A woman is rarely told that her hair is gorgeous freshly washed and unstyled. How rare is the man who steps up and runs his hands through her hair when she hangs her hat on the peg after a long day's work. A woman is rarely told that her fingernails are just as beautiful with little rims of garden dirt under them as they are shellacked and tortured into perfect ovals. We say, "How pretty!" after a process or a long session of alteration. We spend a lot of money and time removing hair from the creases, styling and tinting the hair that is acceptable for viewing.

A woman is rarely told that she is beautiful exactly as she was born . . .

That her whisky laugh

and her natural exuberance

and her morning breath

and her chubby tummy that comes from having borne children

and her unmade eyes

are exactly what a man needs when he wakes up in the morning.

Perhaps a woman must be close to Mother Earth to regain her soul that, early on, gets licked up by the slick flames of magazines full of products to sift her ashes into an acceptable caricature of The Female.

When we first started working cows together, I worried that my lover would think I smelled bad after three nights sleeping out, working hard all day. Maybe he had the same concern. But then we realized . . . we are eating the same foods, bathing in the same winds and campfires, sleeping in the same bag. No worries. Now I crave the natural fibers of sleeping under the moon, no showers, just wood smoke, wool, canvas, horses, wind, dirt . . . a connection with the source that shows me both my female-ness and my male-ness, a tiny penis beneath heavy breasts, a truth that needs not be scented or scrubbed.

For years I was a lopsided child, raising children, focused on some types of conversations, some kinds of information, letting the rest wash over me as a child who plays at the feet of the adults but does not hear the harder truths. I read Nora Roberts and Janet Evanovich but missed Annie Proulx and Terry Tempest Williams, knew all about *respiratory syncytial virus* but nothing of world affairs, measured the ingredients for a thousand recipes but had no idea how to vote. The winter my son was born, I watched the Olympics on television while he nursed, flipping right past the Gulf War. I knew every passionate argument for breastfeeding, cloth diapering, and homeschooling but never considered my consumption of plastics, fossil fuels, or aspartame.

Now, my breasts are empty, leaving room and time for something more than milk.

My baby sister got her ears pierced long before I did. I simply thought it was forbidden. Daddy said no. When she was sixteen, Molly went with my aunt to have holes punched in the lobes of her ears in spite of Daddy. It was many months before I realized that, as a married woman already past twenty years old, I could do with my body as I pleased.

I got my nose pierced when I was thirty-seven. I stood up from a restaurant table in Amarillo, Texas, where my husband had taken me for raw oysters and beer to celebrate my birthday. I stood up and walked out the door, directly into a tattoo shop that reminded me of a medical clinic. I got a cubic zirconia stud in my nose, and I have never taken it out.

As soon as she could after leaving for college, my daughter got her nose pierced, too. The next year she got her first tattoo on the inside of her upper left arm: *Nolite te bastardes carborundorum.* It is in Times New Roman italics.

Never have I been so envious. A few months later I got my first.

We think that our elders will teach us our most valuable lessons. But my daughter has been the one to teach me about being a woman. About how this pretty thing looks different for each of us. About how some of us wear blue eyeliner and some of us don't. About how the call to arms is to lay them down and not fight but to live, to encourage, to love.

I may always be planning my next tattoo. Lily and I exchange e-mails about each piece we are anticipating, saving for, and trying to schedule. Body art has become too complicated to be a drunken mistake. Most shops only accept cash, are booked weeks in advance, require consultations and deposits, and have sign-in procedures that remind me of doctor's office intake forms. They write down your driver's license number. The artists work with their clients via e-mail for weeks prior to putting needle to skin.

I will never again be as young as I am right now, in this moment. I am going to decorate any way I please.

Coming up from sleep, she is a sealed envelope, the narrow entrance to her cave brushed over and hidden and impenetrable, hairy vines barring the way, a slot canyon with moisture way down deep.

Her dreams are full of secrets, little tongues of fire, private proclivities that make her blush in the daytime when she opens the drawer beside the bed to rake the vials of precious oils inside, out of sight.

Her biggest fear is that the springs of wet, the succulence, the pools of shadowed water will never be discovered again, will dry up, will never gush into that geyser of lush again, will sink into the sand never again to rise to someone's bidding.

There are keys to her, unique keys, complicated keys, keys that become more fragile with years, and as your fingers brush from wide crater along sealed crevasse to her burial mound and back, and your tongue does its rote and usual, its tried and true dance, perhaps you will consider springing her open with a little shock . . . a flick of damp into her ear, a grip on her hip that is more firm than tender, a tug on the roots of her hair, a disrespectful shove of your very self up against her belly, a look directly into her eyes, an *open to me, little girl* growled at midnight.

Change the road map. Don't wait on the dark. Hook your finger under her chin or in the top of her shirt and pull her in, coax her, touch her face with hot eyes and hungry hands, make a date on the couch with the first drink, instead of the last, tell her she is naughty, bad, unbelievable, that she has you tangled hopelessly in her hair, and then you will be.

Dig into her sand, shout into her ear with whispers, grind away her tears, bathe in her scent, demand as much as she will give, give what she knows not to demand, and oh, you will be.

My mother has beautiful bones. She pointed out to my daughter, a few months ago, that *she* was the first woman in our family to get a tattoo. She said, "Grammy is way ahead of you," and then pulled aside her blouse to show my child the small black cross on her chest, marking the spot where she had radiation.

I have never been afraid of my mother dying of breast cancer, but I am afraid of torture. I am against torture, even the kind formulated for healing and longevity. A few months after my mother refused her last chemo treatment—there is no magic number—I stood waiting in a small-town airport and watched as an interesting, exotic woman walked toward me through the crowd. My mother! Her very short cap of barely-there hair made her look foreign, elegant, somehow removed from our family of short, dumpy women.

I hope that beneath my skin, I have her elegant bones.

Infinite Pink

I am quite possibly the only cowpuncher who has ever read *Infinite Jest* at cow camp. Not the kind of cow camp with a cabin and Tom Ryan calendar prints on the wall, battered coffee pot on the stove, mouse-chewed blankets on the beds, yellowed Zane Greys on the shelf, but the kind with a wood fire on the ground, a canvas-tarped bedroll, a camp chair, and Dinty Moore beef stew from a can.

Our camp at Cowboy Corral is stashed inside an old gooseneck trailer full of hay. Today I rode the quad to camp so I could re-supply this one and the one located up on the mesa. Our plan is to gather cows out of Weber Canyon for three days. Gail is riding in, leading my horse. I brought a bag of books, a notebook, and three pens. Five eggs wrapped carefully, saved for morning. Two steaks I set out in the sun to thaw.

We tucked a blue tarp around our camp gear in the rear of the trailer when we located it here some weeks ago. Since then, the wasps have moved in, nesting for the fall. And indeed, although the sun is still hot, there is an edge to the daytime air that mimics the rapidly cooling nights. I don't really blame the wasps for their choice until they come boiling hot out from under the tarp. I am less scared of bears than thoroughfares, and I don't normally fight the bees or spiders or even snakes that live where we work, but the red splash of pain on my inner arm makes me run from the yellow jackets that came mad to this day. Two years ago we fought wasps at this set of corrals and I remember a can of poison stashed in the hollow of a tree. I come back armed with my own venom. Not my usual way.

They don't die easily, and the stench almost drives me from the camp as well.

I drag the chairs and the food box, some beer and scotch, a box of pots and pans, curry combs and nose bags out onto the ground. I spread the blue tarp and its corpses in the sun. The air is no longer as beautiful as it was before the war.

I gather wood and let a gentle fire smoke in the afternoon, damp sticks on damp ground. It smells friendly as I drag in more wood, set up our camp with no rush, no urgency now that the wasps are gone. I pick up the big round bedroll by its leather straps and begin cumbersome stepping to the place where we've removed most of the rocks on evenings before. I stop and look high into the trees. Though it is not the season for baby birds, I can hear them chirping. No sign of a nest. I keep going with my burden and the sound goes with me. I think what a shame that something seems to have chewed a hole in our new double sleeping bag rolled inside its canvas tarp. The sleeping bag is hot pink. Rodeo queen red. A joke between us because Gail was so dismayed at the color when we opened the cardboard box when it came in the mail. Sleeps two. Warm to zero degrees, but only if we pull in the sides, because it sleeps two very large people or a community of small ones. And it is pink . . .

But now the silky fabric is rent, the white filling showing through. And emitting chirps. No, not chirps. Squeaks. I spread apart the sides of the hole and peer inside. They are small, blind, helpless, and loud. Sealed-over eyes and useless fingerless hands. Their pale pink spines are curved in not-ready-for-life commas. One by one I pluck them out and carry them back to the trailer, to a place high on the hay bales. I surround them with loose hay and hope the mother mouse returns before they die.

Back home in my office, I am writing a new essay. My editor tells me I have to strike the part about the baby bird impaling himself on a nail, and I argue that it really happened and what about that golden thread of truth? He says that some things are so true they don't translate well to the page.

I wonder if I might write, then, about how we branded that big longear yesterday. His nuts were as big as the steaks at Texas Roadhouse, and the skin popped open pink as they sizzled on the branding pot. They rolled over on their own.

May I write about how much I hate the sound of a dehorning spoon or a night so dark that it took years to shed its evil shuddering from my memory? Both of those things are long past. We don't dehorn on this ranch because we like horned cattle, treasure those cows with natural defenses against the predator: the coyote, the lion, the bear. And my nights are the right kind of dark now. I wear a tank top bearing a quote by the poet Sarah Williams: "I have loved the stars too fondly to be fearful of the night."

May I write about masturbation and menstrual blood, the rich taste of semen, the book my friend wrote that I don't like and how I lied when I wrote him a letter? May I write about the cowboy who told me he likes to call varmints but rarely kills them anymore? He sits in these mountains among the grasses and rocks and lets the foxes, the bobcats, the coyotes come right up to him and look at him curiously. How he likes to be a part of their world, and they are meat eaters just as he is?

May I write about how good that nut tasted as each bite slid down my throat or how Gail left most of his for the ravens because it was still bloody in the middle?

So was mine, but I ate every bite.

And so the day wanes. I sit by my fire, *Infinite Jest* open on my lap, listening for hoof falls in the rock. I examine my inner arm and the fading red welt. I bought this thick book to please someone else, but I find that I am reading it for myself. Even at camp.

We'll drink scotch tonight.

When I finally hear Gail coming, I run to open the gates and unsaddle my horse. He says, "It was nice to smell your smoke as I rode off the hill." We cook the steaks over my coals and read our books by headlamp curled up together in the pink bag.

In the morning, when I open my eyes, Orion is directly overhead, with all his decorations and weapons, glowing and obvious. I turn on my side and see that the campfire is still smoking, tendrils of gray rising into the lightening sky. At exactly 5:00 a.m. the coals burst into flame on their own.

Two Waters Touching

The first person to ever say anything to me about the Marfa Lights was the most unacceptable kid in school. Buddy rode the bus from south of town, and his hair was always shaggy, except for one spring when he was shaved bald after a head lice epidemic in the elementary school. His shoes had holes in them, revealing dirty socks or filthy bare feet. He often wore the same clothes several days in a row and didn't always smell good. On days when the smell was particularly strong he got called out of class by the counselor or the junior high boys' athletic coach. He would be gone for an hour or so and return with wet hair. His hands were hard and dry and cracked, with black under the nails. His cousin came to our school once for about six weeks, and he had one brown eye and one blue eye that was blind because it had been shot out by a BB gun. That had never happened to anyone in my family.

"You've seen them . . . haven't you?" A sneer and a mocking tilt to his head.

He asked this of me, the one who lived on La Caverna, right there on the main highway, right there where his school bus had to pass twice a day, right there in the big house with the red Spanish-style roof, white cinder-block fence, and the ancient pecan trees whose fruits my father shelled with his pocket knife and whose mother made breakfast every single morning and who had to change socks and underwear each night at bath time and whose father threw out the television so that we would do our homework and read books.

But I looked down, kicked a small line in the dirt of the West Texas playground with the toe of my black-and-white saddle oxford, and admitted that I had never seen the mysterious lights and, in fact, my family was Baptist, so I had never even heard of them or the theories surrounding their nighttime appearances on the desert. Theories and mysteries did not thrive inside that white cinder-block fence where the lawn felt as big as a football field sometimes, and the scariest thing was the cactus garden on the outside of the fence. We didn't want to fall to the north when walking the tops of the cinder blocks. My family dealt in fact and truth, the kind translated in King James's time. KJV. Maybe the Amplified, but only when reading for fun.

As I stood in shame before Buddy's question, there blossomed in my white-bread, middle-class chest a longing to ride the school bus to the end of a rural route, to be out after dark under a sky that held such unexplainable phenomenon as lights dancing on the desert. I wanted a one-eyed cousin with the foreign sounding name of Jacques and permission not to take a bath.

La Caverna was really Highway 54, the one that stretched from I-10 all the way up past the Texas/New Mexico border to Whites City where the caverns did, indeed, wait. It might have stretched farther than that, but my map was limited. Our house had four bedrooms and two bathrooms. Right across the highway was my best friend's house, an unpainted gray cinder-block rectangle with a chicken house behind, bare-packed earth all around. There were beds in all the rooms except the kitchen.

My father's ranch truck and my mother's Suburban were parked in front of our house, extra horse trailers in the driveway along the side. The only car ever parked at her house was her father's white city constable car with the lights on top. Her mother did not drive, but instead walked to the grocery store with a little pushcart.

Our house smelled of lemon oil and Pine Sol and whatever my mother was making for dinner while her house always smelled of chiles and tortillas and the open-flame gas heaters that kept every room chokingly hot.

My name was bread-and-butter English, but her first name was Hispanic while her last name was Stanford. I was firmly connected to my side of the street, but somehow she always seemed to be standing in the middle.

At school, she ducked her head and hid behind a curtain of long black hair. We walked home together and she wasn't afraid of the dogs that came barking and snarling out of people's yards the way I was. When I stayed over, her mother made Kraft Macaroni and Cheese in my honor while I longed for the beans and chiles that smelled like heaven.

Here in my mid-forties, I find myself thinking about my mother often, especially in the mornings when I make coffee in the kitchen. I don't think of her if I am making coffee in other places—Willow Springs or camping—only here at the house. For years, my mother drank her coffee with Coffeemate and sugar, a comforting creamy mixture. Then it was Coffeemate and the artificial sweetener of current fad . . . NutraSweet or Sweet'N Low or Splenda, and finally, after breast cancer, stevia.

But though I think of my mother often, I know it is my father who shaped me, made me who I am. Because of him, I try to get on my horse before the boss, lift my end of everything heavy. Because of him I show up to ride all day. Because of him, I know where the coyotes den up.

It is my father's handwriting that spiders across the cover page of my senior research paper. It is because of him that the title is "Think! Said the Monkey," a tongue-in-cheek reference to the Scopes Monkey Trial.

Evolution. Homosexuality. Abortion. Hot topics in the 1980s—and my father was the one who would discuss them.

When I got caught reading smutty novels, he was the one who gave me *The President's Lady*, saying that here was a true love story. And by giving me that book, he gave me all of Irving Stone. *The Agony and the Ecstasy.*

I don't remember her name, though I am sure my mother would if I asked her. The truth is that my mother remembers everyone she's ever met, and she's never met a stranger. I know now that her warning for me to be cautious on our camping trip was offered as the only thing she could think of to say in response to her daughter's crazy scheme of going camping on public land for seven weeks without a plan and with a ten-year-old child in tow. If we had taken my mother along with us, she would have met our neighbors in every campground, gotten their mailing addresses, seen photos of their grandchildren, and found something in common with each one. She would have come gaily back to camp saying, "Did you know that nice lady four tents down is from Midland? She knows my cousin's husband's mother. Very nice people." My mother talks to strangers.

So surely she would remember the name of the foreign exchange student I interviewed for my social studies report when I was in the fifth grade. She was from Cape Town, South Africa, and she told me how the

Atlantic and the Indian Oceans come together at the tip of the country. How you can stand on Cape Point and see the two waters touching, one more green, one more blue. One warmer, one colder.

During the interview, she told me that the biggest difference between living in Cape Town, South Africa, and Van Horn, Texas, besides the obvious absence of ocean, was that we used so many more condiments on our food. Ketchup, mustard, salt, pepper. Tabasco sauce. Pickle relish. A.1. Steak Sauce. Heinz 57. Margarine. Jelly. Syrup. Mayonnaise. Refrigerators full of toppings for our food. Something to make it all better.

A few years ago, over a stiff drink, Ross Knox told me about Two Ocean Creek in Yellowstone National Park, about how when the creek slides off the Divide, one stream flows eventually to the Atlantic and the other to the Pacific.

Just knowing that such a place exists makes it all better.

But Now I Ride

At Cottonwood Spring, there is a tree that sings. Sometimes it is a squeaky gate, sometimes a flute, sometimes a soprano warming up her voice. I am sitting on my horse here in the creek bed, waiting, holding a few cows against the fence until Gail comes along with more. I may be here awhile.

When a woman hires on to cowboy, these are not the moments she anticipates, not the moments anyone talks about. There are no witnesses, no cameras, no glitter, no wild rides with her hair blowing in the wind. No blue ribbons or trophy buckles. No applause and, often, not even an *attagirl*. She's just filling a hole, doing her job.

There are no printed manuals for the job description: cowgirl.

A few months ago, I passed out a survey to a handful of women who have cowboyed for a paycheck. I was not surprised to discover that most of them don't have a strong affinity for the word *cowgirl*. Many of them cited semantics or wryly wrote something about rodeo queens. These women more often think of themselves as cowboys or ranch hands, or simply ranch wives.

But no matter what we call her, she is out there.

She is riding. And digging post holes. Tying in stays. Calving heifers, haying, windmilling . . . often with a toddler in tow. She is cooking over a campfire or in a slow cooker or a cast iron skillet, even after having brought in her share of the cows that day. She's training young horses. Doctoring sick animals. She's riding point or bringing up the drag where all the old grandmas and wobbly new babies linger. She's driving a rig to the sale barn. She is probably complaining about how western jeans aren't made of heavy enough denim anymore, and she won't buy a pair with bling on the back pockets when she rides on them for nine hours a day.

Her gear and tack look much like the men's except for the rubies on the buckle of her chaps. She owns several pairs of work gloves, and she can pull a knife out of her pocket or off her belt if she needs to, perhaps even impatiently if you've been messing around too long trying to pick the tape off a box with fragile fingernails. She can kill a rattlesnake. Fix a water leak and plant a garden. Maybe shoe a horse.

Some women were born into this way of life. Some, as poet and ranch wife Patricia Frolander points out, married into it. Some stepped out onto the path, not following husband or father, but with a strong sense of purpose and choice. Many have had to walk away from the lifestyle through circumstance. But they long for it, identify with being a cowgirl, and will miss it for the rest of their lives.

I came to this job late. I came to this job never having carried a rope on my saddle, never having caught a calf in a loop. I came to this job with the stories of cowboys echoing in my ears and the dough of thousands of batches of bread under my fingernails. I've been a ranch wife since shortly before my twentieth birthday, cooking for cowboys, cleaning up after cowboys, even homeschooling a young man who never wanted to do anything but work with his hands and ride a horse behind a bunch of cows. I've listened to cowboy stories since the day I was born.

But now I ride. I earn my paycheck as a cowboy. Now I spend my share of days in the saddle. All I am doing is learning to see.

I am learning to see the angles and vectors and biology of working cows. I am learning to see when a mama cow has come to the feed ground having left her baby stashed under a tree. I am learning to throw my loop at the same angle as a calf's shoulder and not look at my saddle horn when I dally. I am learning when to make noise and ride hard, and when to back off, be quiet, and give some space to that little heifer who is scared. I am learning to work with my partner in the sorting pen, slow and easy, with more finesse than before. I am learning to trust my horse over the rocks and hold my eyes open during meteor showers no matter how tired I am when I lie down.

Yesterday I rode twenty miles. I rode one horse and led two others into Willow Springs. I dropped the extras in the horse pasture to wait until we come back in a few days, and then turned toward Cottonwood Camp. As I rode, I realized that I am looking forward to cooking over the fire even though my hands will turn black and it will take three washings to get the scent of wood smoke out of my hair when we get home. I am looking forward to eight days without a shower, to two meals a day rather than three, to getting smarter about looking at the ground and knowing what I am seeing as we trail up these cows. I am looking forward to getting stronger as the days go by and being able to get on my horse with ease by the end of spring works.

Perhaps I will even decide to like the word *cowgirl*.

This morning the tree sings soprano in the breeze. I use the first few minutes of my wait to air my horse's back, stretch my legs, take off my coat and tie it on behind my saddle. When I climb back aboard, everything around me stills, and I begin to hear. The creek water gurgles over the rocks. A lizard, wakened early by an unseasonably warm spring, scratches his way through the leaves and along the bark of a tree. A hawk screams from up the canyon, a different scream than the one she'll use when her nest is full of chicks. In a few weeks the lupine and clover will be stirrup high, and I might find some morels in the clearings along the creek banks. I know to watch for a king snake making his way through the rocks, and I'll find a bear track in the sand beside the water.

I can't actually see the cows I am holding through the brush and trees, but I know they are there, bedded down in the shade. I must stay here, in position, blocking the trail out the other side in case Gail brings more cattle from up the creek where he has gone to check the water gap and the bed ground on the ridge. But my girls are here. I saw the red cow lie down through that gap in the leaves and over there I can see the black calf's tail switch from time to time. And just now, one of the cows started licking herself. I can hear each swipe of her rough tongue.

Soon we'll take them along the creek to the corrals and holding trap, picking up any volunteers along the way. It is time to move down the country, down to the desert where the green is carpeting the ground beneath the cedars and mesquites. Where I might see a cactus wren nest in a prickly pear. This is what I do. And this is why I know that at Cottonwood Spring there is a tree that sings.

Eradication

At the confluence of Smith and Cottonwood Canyons a warbler built her nest just upstream from where the black hawk screams above her own. It is a friendly scream. The warbler's elegant nest is in the top of a young cottonwood, and she has stitched slim, tender branches around her small bowl. The black hawk's nest is a junkyard jumble, recycled from last year's ruins.

In the pool between the sandbars, chub and suckers and greenies swim and jostle silently for shelter beneath the rocks. They don't wear name tags saying desirable or un-, native or non-. A giant crawdad with only one claw walks carefully along the bottom. The study of crayfish, crawdads, crawfish is called *astacology*, and the body of a decapod crustacean has twenty segments. What is one missing claw? Its absence doesn't seem to be bothering the granddad moving smoothly along the sand, looking for an unoccupied overhang. He is an invasive species.

I am sitting on a rock, dipping my shirt into the almost cool water, refilling my bottle with water, grateful for water, no matter what swims. The pool and I are baking in the late May sun. It was much deeper when we hiked past here two weeks earlier. Summer has arrived and given up its nighttime hold on spring. The one-armed crawdad and the fish, large and small, are doomed. The hoped-for July monsoons will not get here in time to save them. At first I philosophize about how the dead fish and crawdads will return to the soil, become rich compost, organic matter in the sand, and then I realize that this is not what is going to happen. What is going to happen is that as the water sinks down into the sand and evaporates into the air, as the pool becomes shallow, the crawdads and the fish will begin to make noise, splash around, flop and jump. In their desperation they will give away their location.

As the sun beats down on my back and head, glares off the white boulders, I think of all the creatures who will come to the noise of these pools drying up in the canyon bottoms: black bears, coons, the hawk down the way, foxes, coyotes, and in ancient times, people who made fish jerky, salting and drying it for winter stews.

A few more steps before flesh returns to soil.

Last night we slept just up the canyon, and our heavy packs wait for us there, beside another doomed pool. Doom is the theme of the day. This is the second backpacking excursion we've done this month. The first was four days, three nights, well over twenty miles of extreme boulders and no trails, one of the most incredible experiences of my life. I was challenged and rewarded, awestruck and peaceful, initiated and triumphant. I was the only woman with three men as my companions. Two game and fish experts and my cowboy. It was the first time I've ever been the slowest, weakest hiker in a group. That hike was for surveying, exploration, discovery.

This hike is for eradication.

Three days, two nights, and we've only come two miles. This hike is worth $4000 to the ranch. We've agreed to eradicate.

I now hate tamarisks. The tamarisk, or salt cedar, is a very resilient tree. Like the crawdad, it is an invasive species. Originally planted in the desert by urban dwellers as an ornamental in landscaping or to keep topsoil from eroding, the tamarisk puts down very long taproots and quickly becomes a monoculture in the delicate riparian bottoms of these canyons. I attack each one as if it is the only tree I am going to saw down today, not one of sixty. Or seventy. Groves of tamarisks in the glaring heat of the creek bottom. I particularly hate those that the seasonal floods have tipped over. The downed trunks take root in the messy post-flood mud, and it requires thirty or forty cuts to get all the mini-trunks growing out of the one. Gail is behind me, painting poison on each cut with a brush.

On the first hike, we saw tadpoles in all stages, garter snakes, orioles, a red-spotted toad the size of my thumbnail, leopard frogs. We rescued a young hummingbird who was wet and could not fly until he dried out his wings. Within minutes of being pulled from the creek, he fluttered from my hands and hopped to a perch off the ground and flew away. We found deep pools, walled up from down below, full of naive fish that bit on the lure the moment it touched the water. We photographed and measured each one, throwing it back as soon as possible. The fish quickly stopped biting, naive no longer. They were native roundtail chub, *Gila robusta*, with no invasive non-natives in the pools to compete for food or threaten their young. We saw a pink rattlesnake curled on a boulder in the sun, not to be disturbed, and a very large bull snake who had just shed her old skin, her new skin shining. We heard the zone-tailed hawks high overhead. The fish expert pulled a green sunfish from the creek, removed the hook from her mouth, and threw her casually to the bank, not carefully back into the water as he would have a chub. She was brilliant with spawning colors, gravid with eggs. I looked away as she flopped at our feet, dying in the air. Undesirable.

On this second hike, mostly I am seeing my saw blade. And dirt. And adventitious salt cedar roots. On the first afternoon, I heard a bear splashing through a shallow pool. I climbed up on a rock to see better and watched his high round rump disappear over the bank, moving away from me. Later, as I sawed and sawed and sawed, no end in sight, I doubted what I had seen . . . maybe it was just a black bull. But is a bull less desirable than a bear? Is a chub more desirable than a green sunfish and a toad with red spots more desirable than a bullfrog and a desert willow more desirable than a salt cedar? Is it a matter of who has been here the longest? If so, we should bring back the Prescott culture, those who dried the fish and dug mescal pits during the time the Anasazi were building dwellings in the cliffs to the north. We are the invader, the possible pale-skinned monoculture.

Are the bees eating the grape jelly beside the seed tray back home more desirable than a tanager or oriole who won't pollinate my garden like the bees, but will instead flit on their beautiful way after having dipped their beaks in the sweet, off to raise their young in hidden nests? They wear bright colors. I have stopped putting out seed in the tray this summer because I am tired of feeding the brown-headed cowbirds, those nesting parasites that don't rear their own young and put the warbler at risk. For three years, we've watched a house finch with a large tumor beside his eye come and go with his friends. In the wintertime, I enjoy seeing the chipmunks jump into that same seed tray, their small heads striped just like the white-crowned sparrows. We allow the bull snake to live under the piñon roots by the house, but the back step is stained with the blood of the timber rattler who was sleeping on the mat last summer.

Due to men in suits who sit in offices and discuss ones and zeros and billboards, black and red cattle do better at the sale barn than those of other colors or more colors. We shipped that black bull with white on his belly because many of his calves have white on their bellies, too. I wonder if a yellow steer actually tastes different from a black steer. I am more inclined to believe that their meat is affected by what they eat—acorns and grasses and prickly pear tunas and mahogany blooms—than by the pigment in their hair follicles.

Up on the mesa, a cedar tree removal project is underway. The goal is to remove the trees that are very efficient at sucking up precious water and nutrients, threating to become a monoculture. The hope is to improve the habitat for deer, antelope, and cattle. The hope is to encourage diversity. The hope is to encourage the organic matter in the soil to sprout and grow anew. Side-oats and other grama grasses would be best, but here at the beginning, we are happy to see goldeneye turning the mesa yellow. Goldeneye is a weed—we call it tallow weed. The cows eat it at all stages, from the time it germinates until it dries and the seed heads rattle in the wind. Their shit turns yellow when it blooms.

Late last spring we were sleeping at Cottonwood Corral. We were wrapped in canvas and stars and the music of the creek tumbling over rocks made louder by the dark. The smell of the dying fire scented the air as I dozed off. I woke in the wee hours to the elemental cold and the distant moon. We were sleeping close together and bumped heads when we sat upright too fast in the hour just before dawn, the sound of a baby calf in distress breaking up the dark. He bawled loudly from the direction of the salt ground, but his voice was nothing to his mother's roaring bellow that followed. The eruption of sound made our hearts beat faster with powerlessness. We were helpless in the face of the bovine struggle, the Darwinian fight for survival that must go on each night on this planet, in the wilderness, away from our civilized ears. Maybe our ears are too soft, too far removed from the life/death/life cycle to accept the tight-bagged cow who bawls for three days after the mountain lion feasts on veal, milk-fed. The lion is nursing a den of cubs that she licks in the morning sun when they tumble out to greet her, sniffing the blood on her chin. They are milk-fed, too. Two days later I followed placidly moving cows down the trail when I noticed a spindly-legged black baldy calf with a swollen nose, struggling to breathe, bringing up the rear of the group with a red cow.

Gail said, "Lions try to break a calf's nose first, cutting off his air." He made note of the cow who will always have a home here. Good mother. I am secretly glad he didn't mention the white on her belly and bag.

On the first night of the tamarisk eradication project, we nestled into the sand, a splash of whisky in our tin cups, and listened to the night around us after eating our meal from a foil pouch. Just as it got full on dark, we heard a fox give his eerie mating call, a bit of magic for our sleep. The next morning, I forgot to shake my jeans out before I pulled them on and a scorpion stung me on the hip.

On the second evening, exhausted and discouraged by our lack of progress, I continued to move forward down the creek, sawing every tamarisk along the way without finding a good place for us to stop and camp. It was almost 7:00 p.m. In my fatigue I was not looking ahead so it seemed sudden when I came upon a huge barrier of boulders. On the other side was a deep dark calm pool, calm except for a turtle paddling around, head held stiffly high, looking for bugs. The pool was one that the fish expert from our previous hike would have deemed permanent, though it seems a misnomer in this arid land where water can never be depended on to stay. But the size of the fish I could see from high on the boulders indicated it had managed to stay for some years. The pool seemed walled up on all sides, halting my progress. Beyond it I could see a wide sandbar, perfect for sleeping and cooking and resting, perfect for the night. I took my pack off, laid down my saw, and sat. I sat on a boulder in the evening cool, waiting for Gail to come along from behind, poisoning the stumps of devastation in my wake. As I sat, staring down into the deep water, the turtle surfaced again. I decided that I did not want to know his name, his genus, his species.

When Gail caught up with me, he took off his own pack and sat silently beside me in that pocket of peace. As we sat in the quiet, a way around the pool presented itself. And of course we climbed around and found our sandbar, our home for the night.

After we settled in, I leaned back against my sleeping pad on the sand and watched the hummingbirds feeding on insects and nectar on the rocky, ocotillo-strewn slopes high above us. Down where we were, it was riparian and damp. Up above, desert and dry. As night descended, the hummingbirds changed to bats. Both hungry, both eager, both beautiful, but one desirable to feed in your backyard, one traditionally feared, eradicated from your attic.

Today we have made it to the confluence of the two canyons, to more of the dense stands of salt cedars, to the home of the one-armed crawdad, to the warbler nest high above our heads. Our time is up. We do not have any more Mountain House meals: add two cups of boiling water, wait 8–9 minutes, stir, serves two. We do not have any more days or acres to give to this project. We have come two miles in three days and it takes just under two hours to hike back to Alkaline Spring where the quads wait.

When I get home, a chipmunk has invaded my office, made a big mess by digging the potting soil out of my houseplants, burying M&Ms in the dirt.

Moisture Breeds Moisture

~for John

The beat of the heat is a refrain as we strain toward the hope of rain with dust under our feet and the crust of dried-up ponds mocking the month and the dense blue of the rueful rural sky.

We all say the same thing when we gather, palaver, an old-fashioned word that has seen other dry-fry summers, and I wonder as we stand in the hot wind and slow burn which of these be-hatted men also mourn the loss of lust when the sheet is kicked away by impatient feet and even the early morning is another long slow wait, grate, uneasy fate, gray slate of un-puffed sunrise, then red red red.

There is no poetry in July.

Old timers talk of monsoons, coming always soon, thunderstorm noons, but no clouds until midday tunes on the radio.

Sweat dampens the bottom layer of my hair and the cold beer in my hand doesn't stay cold, and the conversation is getting old, chances sold, may I lay my livestock cards down, fold, hold instead the aces of *weather worries are for peasants*, for drought stories already told, Steinbeck.

Even these old men look bewildered and hopeless as we speak of shipping cows before they get too thin.

Drought, that period when nothing is happening. When the soul and the body and the land are barren, arid, lacking. When touching a paintbrush, or an idea, or his hand takes too much energy. When the wind blows and the land and the heart are scoured with loneliness. When the thought of making love seems ludicrous and foreign, when legs and arms and lips stay folded and tight, when the kiss is dismissive at the beginning of the night. When coffee is the most sensuous thing in her day. When popcorn clouds hang motionless in blank blueness and the sunrise is an unforgiving flame. When we begin to doubt the seasons. When mundane tasks are an analgesic, dulling the echo of previous loves and projects and crops. Perhaps even future choices.

Hope is a black-bottomed cloud in the southwest, an almost imperceptible shift in the wind, the feedstore jest that it always rains right after a dry spell. Hope is the beginning of a tear in her eye, a break in the bleakness of her expression, and even she misses the first dampness that seeps from the depths. It can't be called humidity yet, just a heaviness in the air, a rearranging of the dusty canvases and a shuffling of the tubes of color, a deep sigh as she turns over in her sleep, her legs moving with a restlessness previously absent. A pull to vigil, a watching of the sky.

The storm is not always violent. The lightening does not always strike. But, she walks with a sway and her smile has a certain quality, a connectedness to her breathing. The rain may come in torrents, running off in a plowing, coffee-colored rush, or it may come one drop at a time, scenting the air with miniature puffs of dust. He lifts his head at the sound, at the smell, at the taste of *it's finally here.*

Her eyes sparkle, hinting at the pool between her thighs, for she's fully aware now. The lid is off, the season shifts, and the colors are tentatively mixed, the old with the new, the damaged with the fresh.

Toadstools, like flirtations, begin to spring up, evidence of life and fertility; they are useless, inedible, just the frontrunners of possibility . . . for moisture breeds moisture. The artist dips clumped dry brushes in water, in paint, stirring, mixing, wondering, looking, pausing, hesitating and yet, burgeoning with the vision.

Someone Else's Tree

I am turning my shoulder to the calendar, practicing not noticing as the days slip by. As of October, I will have lived here, in one place, for five years. As of November, I will have broken my lifetime record. I look away, again, from the calendar.

The house finch is an indiscriminate nester. Every spring I walk out to the horse trailer several times a week and pull nesting material from the gooseneck. We've learned the hard way that she cannot be trusted, cannot be discouraged. She will build, and build again. We've tried to move her nest of eggs to a nearby tree. It never works. She can never find it, and when we pull back up to the barn to unload tired horses, her eggs will have been eaten or destroyed.

Until I was thirty-eight years old, I moved at least every five years, sometimes as often as eighteen months or six months. I moved at the whim or the dictates of a man . . . my father or my ex-husband. Life is a spiral dance, and we come full circle, back around to where we were but it is never the same and we are never the same. Today I find myself, once again, living in a house that belongs to someone else, on a ranch working for wages, nesting in someone else's tree.

Every spring I pull nesting material from the gooseneck. Every spring, and this spring makes five.

This is the time of year that the swallows clean house, sweeping the eggshells from their nests. The wild green grapes are gone, devoured at first sugar by so many.

I want to pick up the eggshells, but I am oh, so careful, for the lightest touch can crush. They aren't chickens.

"But they are already broken," you say.

"I know, but I can't bear to be the one who does any more damage."

Late at night, in the dark, we are speaking of the past and he says, "Don't touch that."

I nod with respect, for I know how fragile *already broken* can be.

He made me sad even before I knew his name: Common Snipe. He waded all day in the edge of the water, dipping his beak again and again into the mud, seeking snails and worms. He was so intent on his work that I could come right up close if I knelt down. He stayed at the dirt tank for as long as we were camped there, and maybe even after we were gone. I'll never know.

"Don't snipes have mates or are they always alone?" Gail asks me this because before I arrived on the Spider, he saw only birds, little gray birds, LGBs, rather than individual species. He knows I will look it up. I find that the male snipe puts on a spectacular display during the mating ritual, almost suicidal in its frantic necessity. Perhaps because he is alone the rest of the year.

Stocky, small wader native to the Old World. I suppose one reason I like him is that describes me, too. Dipping for sustenance in the mud along the shore, no matter if that shore is in the desert, a long way from the pavement.

When I was pregnant with my first child, the older women on the ranch spoke of the nesting instinct, about knowing labor was near when an expectant mother started cleaning everything in sight and folding tiny onesies, stacking them in tippy columns. What they didn't realize was that I had been nesting my whole life. As the time for my son to be born approached, I walked for miles on ranch roads, making my nest in the wind. The onesies had been folded months before.

As a little girl, I played house in the noses of long horse trailers, begging my mother to let me sleep in them on summer nights. On hot afternoons, I crawled along the high part of the cinder-block wall to the place where the ivy hung from an old tree, shielding the fence from sight. I scooted my books and water and dolls and pillow up under the canopy, creating a place to be alone and hidden. Sometimes I made my castle on top of the shed tucked into the corner of the backyard, its flat roof the perfect place to sit in the sunset or watch the neighbors' fireworks on the 4th of July. I made houses in the hot sandy alley using railroad crossties as walls. My sister had the house next door and we made a path between thresholds, never stepping through the walls. I remember once playing house out in the desert around Chispa. My sister and one of our friends and I used the windblown sand ridges as walls, tucking rocks and sticks up under the mesquite trees, our natural kitchens. Recently Gail and I drove through Chispa between Van Horn and Valentine, on our way to Alpine, and I wondered, "What does *chispa* mean?" Spark. Those long-time-ago girls from my memory were little sparks of women running around in the desert, playing wife and mommy and homemaker.

I continued to nest even after I was past little girlhood, excited each school year by the neat number etched on the door of my locker, my new address. I taped photos and class schedules and cuttings from magazines to the gray walls, hung friendship bracelets from the coat hooks, wished for a man.

My sister and I loved cleaning our bedroom, moving all our belongings out into the hallway—much to our mother's dismay and inconvenience—and then putting everything back, one item at a time, carefully, thoughtfully, in place. We called these events *All Out, Clean Outs.*

I got a house to keep, and a man, much sooner than I expected. I nested in camp house after camp house, from ranch to ranch, always cleaning up the dirt from the people before and mopping my way out the door when the trailers were loaded again. I learned to wrap fragile things, dishes and knickknacks, in sheets and towels, packing and unpacking boxes again and again.

I made jokes about how my husband and my father didn't have much in common except their hobby . . . moving.

I bought a new broom for each house because someone told me it was good luck. *All Out, Clean Out.*

I finally stopped nesting in houses. I stopped moving for men. I lay on the floor in a fetal position in a cold dark dungeon up on a hill, waiting until it was time to nest again. Dormant until the time was right.

There is nothing left of my childhood in my parents' home . . . no outgrown toys, no worn-out tennis shoes, no scruffy teddy bears, no high school yearbooks.

My parents have moved often since I was born, even more freely since their four children moved out, and have perfectly plausible explanations about where it all went. But I miss the framed Tom Ryan calendar prints that hung in the dining room when I was a small child. *Sharing an Apple*. I miss the patchwork rug with my name inlaid where I played as if each section were a room in my doll's house. I miss that copy of *The Complete Sherlock Holmes* that took up my whole summer when I was fourteen.

I miss the shiny blue ceramic snail, the chipped black Cocker Spaniel sculpture that Dad always said reminded him of his first dog, Jazbo, the funny burnt orange rocking chair, the taped-together boxes of Springbok jigsaw puzzles, the tin butterflies that hung over the toilet in several bathrooms as we moved from house to house. They were tacky, but I miss them.

My mother sold all her wedding pottery in a garage sale, Antique Grape pattern, the one I spent months searching for on eBay so that I could give her replacement pieces on her birthday and Christmas one year.

My father's horseshoeing equipment is stored in my brother's garage and my great-grandmother's dolls have been missing for years.

At the Arizona-Sonora Desert Museum, the hummingbird nests in the newly built aviary kept falling apart. Jelly-bean eggs and fragile chicks tumbled to the ground. The puzzled scientists and distressed volunteers stood in the netted enclosure discussing nutrition, territorial behaviors, vegetation, and experienced versus inexperienced nesters. There were no successful nests that first year, only frantic hummers building inefficient nests. One evening a volunteer stood in her own backyard watching an Anna's wind spider web around her beak, over and over again. In imitation, she wound web around some sticks and carried them into the aviary.

The scientists introduced spiders into the environment they had created. The next spring, almost all of the nests were successful, held together by the tensile strength and flexibility of arachnid/hummingbird symbiosis.

The man who built my saddle is dead now, robbed of old-man-hood by cancer. He measured me carefully, hosting me there in his shop in Claude, Texas, while he formed the ground seat. It is a simple western saddle built on a ladies' California roper tree, no fancy stamping on the rough-out leather. Because I am less than five feet tall, it looks ridiculous on a horse. It has never hurt a horse's back though, and now it has the wear of miles on it. When I was guiding guests and leading a string of pack mules in the eastern Sierras, I hung a canvas nose bag from the saddle horn. After some practice I could eat lunch, take photographs, and drink from my water bottle as I rode down the trail, five in hand. Here on this ranch, I tie my coat on behind when the day heats up. I coil my rope up small so my thigh rests beneath it. My gloves are tied beside my left knee and a handsaw and some wire cutters are tied inside a Levi-leg behind the cantle. My favorite recent addition is a bull bag over the horn. I asked Gail, "How long until the hair sloughs off?" He said, "Depends on how much you pet it!"

My phone fits in my shirt pocket when I ride and after last week the memory card is full of wildflower photos. We saw snakes, a million tadpoles, deer, pinch bugs shaped like fallen leaves nestled in the mud of the stream, a baby calf as it took its first steps, two bulls duking it out instead of doing their jobs, laurel blooming in the canyons, a bear track bigger than my hand, a lion track with a cub print alongside, and a Gila monster who hissed when I tried to take his portrait. My favorite flowers here in the Santa Maria Mountains are the mariposa lily and the sego lily.

The grand old house is beginning to settle and sink, to wrinkle and sag. Her bones creak and everything is out of date except the six-pack of pale ale someone stashed in the fridge. She needs new insulation and window sashes, perhaps even new windows. The better to see you with, my dear. She doesn't have Wi-Fi and her radiator is fitful, her plumbing tender. Memories and ghosts speak loudly inside her walls, and when I go in there alone, I try not to disturb them. I tiptoe. She smells of old books, old pages, and old rugs now rather than cigarette smoke or long-loved recipes coming out of the oven or hair tonic. An old tree leans precariously, contemplating the comfort of lying down on her roof, away from the ever-increasing noise of the street. The painting of the cowboys roping the devil hangs above the mantle in the living room. Buster Jig and Sandy Bob, with the devil forever subdued.

Everyone in this family has their mail delivered to the old house, even those with houses of their own, houses on streets inside the city limits, mailboxes. They say, "We've always gotten our mail at Granny and Papa's house." Why would they do it any differently now? The address is known, comfortable, familiar, rightful, a shorthand designation for home, for a place where they grew up, played poker, knew what Christmas would bring, listened to stories and poems, even the boring parts, knew their own history. Now my son Oscar uses this mailing address as well. They are right. It is easier that way.

She is an old woman with a broad lap, ancient breath in our ears, and if we listen closely, something to say.

Tonight we will sleep once again on a sandbar beside a pile of bear scat. This is the second night of a three-night backpacking trip through some of the deep canyons on this ranch. I am sitting on a damp inflatable pad, my wet clothes and shoes spread on rocks above me to dry, a novel, a pen, a blue Moleskine journal, a headlamp and a wool hat in a neat pile beside me. We eat our dehydrated meal from cunning tin plates. Tonight it is chicken teriyaki with rice. I'll tuck my fork and spoon back into the top of my pack tomorrow morning after I drink a cup of coffee made from a slim tube of instant coffee grounds and rinse my plate in the stream.

Carrying my house on my back comes easy to me even if later in my life. As I lie on the sand, I can't help but feel triumphant. Today I found myself swimming through deep water between high cliffs, pushing my pack balanced on the sleeping pad ahead of me through the water. Careful not to dump my house, not to lose what few things I have with me, careful not to upset the balance. Like a turtle, I am a slow hiker, my center of gravity compromised. But I am also more free than I have ever been. I may choose any sandbar to sleep on. And I think the bear will share.

Someone gave me a T-shirt that says, "Camping is in Tents." What is intense is getting a divorce and being homeless. What is intense is running out of spider web. What is intense is watching my daughter's horse fall all the way down on his side on a slab of slick granite in the backcountry of Yosemite all because she is following her crazy mother. What is intense is discovering new love. What is intense is having teenagers. What is intense is no longer cooking for cowboys while listening to cowboy stories, but learning to do the job myself, doing the work. What is intense is the recognition that the journey we are on is of our own choosing—that everything that has come before has prepared us for where we are now.

When I got to this ranch and this love, I began collecting bird nests of all kinds. They line the shelves of our living room. The oriole's nest made of horse hair and hay twine is from a morning in Texas when I made Oscar climb a tree and cut it down before I drove away from him, back to Arizona. I had to move some books to make room for all my nests. I even have a book to help me identify the types of nests built by the different species of birds here in this migration corridor. My mother always said not to pick up bird nests because they are full of lice, but I found a website that says to microwave a nest on high for two minutes and nuke the little suckers. We don't have a microwave in this kitchen, but there is one in the bunkhouse down at the barn.

On one shelf, beside my father's horseshoeing and hoof anatomy books, there is a hummingbird's nest, still attached to the branch, collected after the fledglings flew. I found it while I was horseback, at just the right level to see the newly hatched babies, the size of my pinkie nail, within its contours. I went back every day until they flew. It is flexible, expandable, able to adapt as the chicks grew. I don't think I will put it in the microwave.

The bull bag on my saddle horn is slick. I am home.

The Black Hen

I don't have any close friends here, in Arizona. In the last several years I've met many people. After all, I am in a relationship with a man who was born in the local hospital and whose grandfather was the first postmaster of the township. We occasionally dine in the old building downtown that housed his great-grandfather's mercantile at the turn of the century. His grandmother took advantage of the Homestead Act on a piece of ground to the southwest. My new last name is recognized. "No, I am married to one of his sons."

Any roots I've ever had were fragile and tentative, ripped from the soil with two weeks' notice. Difficult to want to plant a garden or a rosebush. Or change my name again.

My daughter suggested I look on meetup.com for a group to join. My pores shrank in defense. It is a long way to town and all. Still, someone to meet for coffee and girltalk. . . .

I'd like to be friends with my tattoo artist, but she's really busy. I follow her on Instagram instead.

I have a little black hen, one of several chickens given to me last fall. She's one who survived the coyote massacre of mid-winter—and, in fact, has spent several nights alone in the woods. Chickens are herd animals, but as such, they are also very cruel. They will peck horribly at anything red. They are drawn to the color of blood, to any show of weakness within the flock. This little hen must have gotten injured, perhaps by the rooster. Shall we discuss rape in the natural world (or un-natural since domestication is involved)? Anyway, whatever happened, the other hens and the rooster began attacking the black hen any time she came down off the roost onto the hen house floor. Soon she had no feathers on her back or neck, and her head was bloody, one big oft-broken scab.

Since my management of the poultry is decidedly laissez-faire, I pretty much shrugged and said I'd let nature take its course—a hypocritical stance for someone who keeps hens for eggs. Nature has little to do with it.

The black hen began flying over my head and out the open door any time I went into the hen house to gather eggs and tend to chicken chores. She'd spend a few days in the woods on the hillside before showing back up, asking to be allowed back in with her abusers. After all, they had food and water, even if she had to endure a beating to partake. I think she got lonely out there among the grass and leaves.

Sleeping alone.

Early in spring, things changed. One of the brown hens went broody, and I set up a dog kennel in the hen house to allow her to hatch out a clutch of eggs while still being part of the community. One day, while I was tending to this additional chore, the black hen flew over from her safe perch on the roost to stand on top of the kennel. I put water and food for her there, in safety. When I left, she had been eating and drinking for over ten minutes without pause.

Every day I make sure the black hen has food and water up high where no one can beat her up. In fact, I think the other chickens have forgotten she exists, above their heads. Chickens don't look up.

Yesterday, I worked all day, horseback, sorting cattle in the heat. When the second load of shippers left for the sale, the evening settled into relative silence, only cows bawling for missing children, dogs panting in the heat, a hawk screaming. The world endured the slowly cooling heat. Evening came on with chewing horses. Chore time.

I trudged to the chicken pen with a bucket of water dragging on one arm, a bucket of hay scraps so much lighter on the other. The second broody hen of the year sat still on her eggs in the dog kennel. The mean brown hen led her teenager chicks from one exciting scratch to the next. Everyone gathered around the fresh water, drinking with eyes closed.

The black hen came close to me as I filled her water container and scooped feed into her dish. As I set the dish back on the kennel, she hopped onto my arm. The black hen perched on my arm. I stood very still. The black hen began, not to gulp her food, but to rub her poor scabbed head gently on my shoulder. The little black hen stood on my arm and rubbed her head affectionately on my shoulder.

I am her only friend.

This morning I put salve on her scabs and she allowed me to stoke her ugly featherless back and neck. This morning I gave her the choice bruised grapes and slimy salad scraps. This morning I made sure her water dish was fresh and sweet.

I am her only friend.

Taking Census

There are three houses at Spider Ranch headquarters, as well as an enormous barn and a bunkhouse. The census takers who drove out, forty-five minutes from town, were stunned. I am not sure if they were stunned to find that two people live out here or that only two people live here. They kept asking, "Who lives in that house? Well, then, who lives in that one? Who lives in the one with the huge doors?" Um, hay. Alfalfa lives in the one with the huge doors. And the bats. And cats. The census takers came out a total of five times. To figure us out. To count us. To count the persons.

I suppose it does seem like a lonely place to live if one is accustomed to stores and crowds and sirens and traffic and a quick pizza when dinner is late. But at times, our lives seem crowded, even this far from town.

We listened to *This One's For Him*, the Guy Clark tribute album, while we buried Sophie. Jim was too little then to jump in and out of the truck by himself, so he sat on the lowered tailgate and waited breathlessly for one of us to absently rub his ears.

There are times in life when we must move with a carefully straight spine and breathe shallow breaths, as if enduring a headache, because to breathe too deeply or move too broadly is to bump into pain—acid pain. If we are truly living, those times are unavoidable.

Cooper was an old shepherd-looking dog—a good cow dog even if he was just a mutt. Maybe he had some McNab in him. Gail inherited Cooper and the little red dog, Jake, when Bill Murphy died. He promised Bill that these friends would have an always home.

2008 was a hard year of uncertainty and work. A year of upheaval and earthquake.

2008 was a brilliant year, a year of falling in love, of recognition, of *oh, there you are!* Late in the year, we came together—moved stiffly through the days to avoid the acid pain of loss and intrusion and change. We rested only in the love-filled darkness, recharging for the day coming again. But earthquakes require reconstruction. And none of us exist in a vacuum; we function within families, communities, in relation to others, the earth, the weather, our animals.

I complained to Gail that Jake didn't like me. Gail said, "Of course he does," and then smirked. We all know who the alpha is around here.

That was before Purrl.

Our reconstruction involved teenagers with confused and lonely eyes . . . one who refused to dismantle a childhood's worth of Lego structures and one who sat defiantly on the arm of the couch and dared us to form a unit opposite her. Our reconstruction involved making simple decisions about where to sleep. We were spread out awkwardly over two houses, neither one home to me.

I opened the door to the master bedroom and gazed at the piles of Gail's belongings on the floor, the dirty fuzz-filled rectangle where the bed had stood before his separation from his wife of twenty-three years, and shut the door again. It was a few more weeks before I went in armed with a broom. When the room was ready, I got in the truck with Gail and we drove to the barn to get a bed out of storage. The dogs ran alongside, old Cooper stumbling to keep up. We got the bed loaded and turned back toward the house only to realize that there in that day already filled to the top with pain, Cooper was dead beside the road. His heart hadn't kept up.

He wasn't my dog.

Sophie died in the deep hard winter two years ago, the same winter Jim came to stay and then live. She was a gray-and-white Catahoula. Jim is a Blue Lacy cross, maybe too short-haired for these mountains, but way tough and fast enough. He is joyous enough. Jake, old and stumbly himself now, is at my heels every step when Gail is away but reverses his affections the moment Gail returns home. Ellie simply comes along, fat and happy, barking in all the wrong places, at all the wrong people. Gail keeps threatening to give her away, but I don't think he means it. Jake must be lifted into the back of the truck now, and when we go on a long quad ride, he rests on an old saddle blanket on the back of Gail's quad. Jim can run for miles and miles, hours and hours, bounding high to see over the bushes. He's too young to get tired and footsore.

The ranch bought three fillies from the O RO Ranch: Bonnie, Linda, and Penny. One day as we rode up the lane, they ran to the cross-fence to greet us. I exclaimed, "Gail! That mare is bred!" He scoffed. "No way. She is just an easy keeper." Penny gave birth to a bonus baby around Halloween, a catch colt named BB. The old mares in retirement, Brownie, Punkin', and Bumper, acted as doting aunties. The day after BB was born, they brought her and Penny across the grassy flat at Old Camp, flanking them in a chevron pattern, presenting them to us, mother and daughter. The three old mares are gone now.

Roscoe is the big white horse I like to rope on in the branding pen. Ivan is fun to sort on, but is sometimes too aggressive, even once, last fall, whirling to kick a yearling back from the gate. Scout is our problem child, but even problem children age and mellow. Luna's earned her right to be a bitchy old matriarch. After all, the old mares, especially Brownie, kept her in line when she was young. Recently we drove to the RO Ranch for two new fillies. I was determined to let the ranch owner, Gene, name these new girls, but within a few weeks we were calling them Birdie and Little Red while we taught them to eat grain from nose bags and load in the trailer with no fuss.

Gail and Linda had a wreck right after she got here, a wreck that included a load of salt on a pack horse, a rope under Linda's tail, and a low-hanging limb that Gail did not quite make it under. But now she is one of the team. Bonnie was scared of her shadow, but now that she's realized that she's higher in the pecking order than the cows, she is gaining confidence. Recently we sat beside Horseshoe Tank at sundown and ate our dinner by the fire while she herded the cows out the gate and into the night trap, almost completely on her own, shaking her head like a snake when one of the cows looked back.

Jim keeps all the ravens off the ground. No jackrabbits allowed in the open area between the house and the barn. Jake would love it if I'd let the hens free-range, not so he can kill a chicken but so he can help me gather eggs. His coat would look lovely, but we'd be eating oatmeal for breakfast. When their owners go on vacation, Duke and Mary or Buddy or Sonora come out to spend a week at the ranch. That is a lot of dogs.

Last fall we shipped the old white cow. She was the last cow on the ranch Gail didn't have a hand in branding. He stopped at the gas station on his way to the sale, and when he stepped out of the store, walked toward the truck and trailer, she heard his voice, turned her head, and bawled in recognition. We put the Dog-Hater cow through the gate at Saddle Tank the other day, and we saw the Earth Mother down around Elbow Spring. The old hooky cow doesn't even have a baby at her side right now, but she shook her head at us when we took her through the gate at the salt. Her daughter has inherited her hooky trait and she hasn't even given birth yet. She doesn't faze Linda a bit, but Penny doesn't know what to think of a cow that acts like that.

Eyebrows was already grown before he ever saw a man on a horse.

The little longeared bull took a dive off into the boulders just before we got to Willow Springs. "Just ignore him. Act like we don't care what he does." We took the rest of the group to the corrals, threw out fragrant flakes of alfalfa, and began our evening chores. "Oh, Gail. Look." The little black bull with white commas above his eyes had jumped over the barbed-wire fence, happy and secure and eating, back with his clan. Eyebrows is a full-grown turnout bull now, huge and gentle and willing.

Gene brings feral cats out from town, but cats are harder to locate than cows. None of them have stayed in the sunny courtyard of the big house on the hill. I feed three on the windowsill behind my office while Gail feeds two more moms with litters in the hay at the barn. We can pet the long-haired calico. In fact, she demands it.

A boar coon keeps eating the cat food up on the haystack. Gail tried securing it by rolling the top of the bag. In retaliation, the coon shit on the bag, knocked the ladder over, and killed the barn rooster. Gail declared vengeance by baiting a HavaHart trap. All he caught was a wild tom one night and Jim the next. Jim got to eat the sardine bait but had to spend a cold night in the trap before we discovered he was missing.

The bull snake that lives in the roots of the juniper hatched out baby bull snakes. One of them fell on my hat when I opened the barn door. I tipped my head forward, and he dangled in a long line from the brim until he dropped to the ground and slipped away into the wood pile.

Jim went missing on the opening day of deer season last fall. Gail and I were at Willow Springs, gathering cows. Gene put an ad in the paper, a notice on Craigslist, and called the Humane Society. When we rode in to headquarters several days later, I was prepared for him to be gone, prepared for only the old dogs to come running to greet us. Still, tears clouded my vision as I unsaddled. My dog was gone. The next day we drove to the shipping pens, stopping on the flats where several hunters were camped.

Heather opened the door to her RV and Jim came running out. I said, "Jim. Get in the truck." Heather told Gail all about how Jim likes to play with her children and how they let him sleep in the RV at night so he wouldn't be cold. I told her, "He has a heated dog house." When I hugged him later, Jim smelled of Heather's perfume.

Driving home from town at dusk, we saw a terrible flapping scuffle in the middle of the narrow blacktop. I convinced myself it was a large bird of prey with a small animal in its talons. As we drew closer we saw that it was not a bird at all, but a wrestling match between two small badgers, possibly littermates. Their battle was loud and vicious and lopsided. One was definitely getting his ass kicked. We sat and watched, stunned both by what we were seeing and the noise. Badgers are loud. Finally, the one who was, it seemed, winning, saw us and let go of his brother to run off into the weeds by the side of the road. The almost-doomed badger got up off the pavement, and thinking he had routed his attacker, shook himself, stiffened his front legs and gave aggressive hops. He made teenage-boy *huh, huh, huh* sounds in the direction his brother had fled. As if. As if he were quite the stud. Then he turned and saw us. *Huh, huh, huh!* He postured at us as well, expecting applause I suppose. We laughed. If I ever own a sports team, I want the badger to be the mascot. The Fighting Badgers. The Santa Maria Fighting Badgers.

Another time as we drove home in the dusk, we saw a bobcat chasing a rabbit. Several times we have watched elk butts disappearing into the night. In the fall, Swainson's hawks gather on the grasslands to eat grasshoppers before flying to Argentina. And once, a snowy owl.

One evening, we rode to Willow Springs. The last leg of the trail is very steep. We had a bet going about whether or not there would be cows in the lower horse pasture since the motorcycle cattle guards on the quad trails are shallow and ineffective. I looked up the hillside (now known as Little Bear Hill) and said, "There is a black . . ." I was going to say "cow," but instead said, "bear!" And sure enough, a small bear, probably a yearling, was on the slope high above us. As we sat there watching him, he chased—and caught—a jackrabbit. Jim is very fast, and I see him chase jackrabbits every day, but he never catches one. This little bear caught his quite handily and then, walking stiff-legged to keep it from dragging the ground, carried it over to where there were, indeed, a few of our cows, and plopped down with them to eat his meal. When we got to the spring, we could see by the manure, scat, and tracks around the water that the little bear had been living with those cows for quite some time.

The calico cat in the haystack had four kittens. One is yellow, one is calico, one is gray and one is gray tabby. I picked up the gray one when they were balls of hissing spitting fur. Gail said, "Don't ruin them!" so I handed her to him. Oh, so soft. We really did try not to handle them much so they would stay wild. In early December, though, Gail came to breakfast and said, "If you don't do something that gray kitten is going to die." The kittens were way past weaning, and the other three were thriving. The gray one seemed injured in her back, possibly by the coon, and was both starving and lacking the ability go to the water trough for a drink like the rest of the cats. In fact, that morning, when Gail went to feed the horses, he found her down in the dirt. The dogs surrounded her, and she was too weak to run away. Hollering at the dogs to stay back, he lifted her little sack of bones back up to safety on the hay.

Midmorning, I walked to the barn through the cold December wind. I tucked the thin little cat in the front of my coat and carried her to the house. She didn't struggle. For three days, she didn't leave the laundry basket. She sat shivering, only moving to eat or drink enormous amounts of water. She slept curled up by a hot water bottle that I re-heated often. On day four she began hopping out to explore, to use the litter box, to attack our feet. The policy around here has always been No Animals in the House. I write this in mid-January with Purrl in my lap, sleek and round and healthy, saved by canned cat food and love. She kills our snow boots every evening and sleeps at the foot of our bed until early morning when she walks the length of my body to put her nose on my nose.

Recently, Japan and other countries declared dolphins to be non-human persons. Given the population around here, there are many persons that are non-human. I am content to simply be one in a number of persons that thrive in this community. There are some statistics that the census numbers will never show.

BLM

Jesus loves the little children . . . red, brown, yellow, black and
white, they are precious in His sight.
~Sunday School children's song, words by C. Herbert Woolston

My maternal grandfather has his initials tattooed on the inside of his right forearm. *BLM*. He is a veteran of WWII so I never asked him about the splotched black ink, assuming he got it while in the service. Our assumptions lead us astray, especially our assumptions about story and belonging and beauty. Only recently did I hear Granddaddy Bill tell about when the carnival came to West Texas and he helped the carnies set up on a small-town vacant lot. They offered to pay him with either $10 or by tattooing his initials on his arm. The wound got infected, and boy, was his mother mad. He was twelve years old, in the middle of a Great Depression.

The storytellers in my family rarely have the opportunity to use the word *carnies*.

A woman who is writing a book came out to the ranch to interview me. She is intrigued by what she calls *ranch women*. She assumes we all fit inside the box she has designed for us. She asks my opinion about a recent story in the news, one involving guns, *surely I am pro-guns*, a siege, a debate centered around land, now a death. Someone on one side shot someone on the other. Extra, extra, hear all about it. There are always sides.

The words *cowboy* and *rancher* shouted by the media have defined us with a narrow and inaccurate lexicon, like being inside a funhouse full of mirrors that twist our image into something we are and yet we are not. She wants to know about our dealings with the BLM. I reply that we work with many people within many government agencies: the AZGF, NRCS, NFS, but not the BLM. She insists the BLM, the Bureau of Land Management, controls all of the public grazing in the USA. She is infected with propaganda and misinformation.

I cannot allow her to tell my story.

The news continues to roll across our country, though I am not sure that we are getting the true news. I am perched precariously, half on the back of a chair, half on a windowsill that is almost as wide as my foot. The window screen is pushed aside so I can take a photograph of the cat-faced orb weaver who has built a gorgeous web under the overhang of the roof. She is the queen of trapeze artists for she spins her own. She is magnificent . . . orange and yellow and brown with the deceptive face, a clown's evil smile, tattooed on her abdomen. I post the photograph on social media, telling her story, her news. It never occurs to me that someone might find her frightening just because she is different from them, that someone might adopt a scorched-earth policy against her kind, creatures with eight legs rather than two. Her life matters, as least to her. At least to me. I continue to assume that everyone will find her beautiful and understand why she belongs here.

I assume you understand me when I speak, but now I don't know what to say. Our summer is assaulted with more bad news. More screaming from the brightly lit screen. More bloodshed in the dust. More violence. More talking-head barkers standing in the fairway of the news feed, waving us over, telling us to look this way, *step right up and see the horrible show*, a distraction from our depressing lives. See the attractions, the bearded truth, the two-headed illusion. More polarization. More wounds. More divide, even within our own family. None of us have caught a bullet yet, and I can't pray hard enough for those other families. Red, brown, yellow, black, and white. Our nation is saturated with more capital letter designations to keep us from hearing each other, seeing each other, touching each other in love, melting together. We can't decide if life matters or if we should stay silent about what matters. We are infected with fear and misunderstanding.

There will be scars to mar the beauty we were meant to be.

Wild Things

Yesterday I saw a praying mantis, in defensive position, ready to box atop a dried cow pat—only nothing was dry and all that had been was no longer. Only forty-five minutes before, we'd dismounted under a spreading cedar tree, donned our slickers and sheltered on the lee side of our horses, our backs to the storm, our hats tilted forward to let the rain run off the brims. First came glassy jewels of hail the size of juniper berries and just as blue. Then came driving sideways rain and the ground began to run and move and designate its low places and its high. Animal and man endured. Endurance of that sort is the kind of no choice. Not brave, not heroic, not lauded—just a stoic making it through.

When the downpour and bright sheets of lightning moved past, we rode on, taking the cows with us. When we got to the gate they must go through, the whole world was one large mud, and the light was filtered so that everything seemed highlighted. In the middle of the task, I saw the brilliant green mantis. Her drying out was disturbed by the cows moving around and atop her world. Her dukes were up.

I wanted to take a photograph but there was no time so we kept going, convincing the cows to take the gate—but I remember her—her green and her upraised forearms, and I hope she lived. I hope she lived to fight and pray another day.

I dreamed last night of tiny, jewel-toned tree frogs resting on my pulse points, miniature sea creatures that had been dormant for years coming to life in the creases of my days, vulnerable wet things that begged to be saved.

I saw a two-tailed lizard on the wall last week.

The bats have flown down to Mexico early, and the hummers are tanking up on sugar, preparing to meet them there. I keep finding piles of acorns hidden beneath brush stacks, tarps, feed sacks, and I wonder who is storing them, and why so many? The air has an edge this morning, a warning, a fission of chill that is playful, gleeful, and yet, tired. My slicker and my jacket are tied on behind my saddle, and I tuck a burrito in my saddle bag.

It is a good year for acorns.

I spend the winter wanting to live with wild things until I become a wildish thing.

If I ever find the perfect digging stick for wild onions, I am going to keep it forever. I will leave it to my daughter who will find it among my things, and sigh and wonder about her weird mother. Or perhaps she will not sigh, but will put it in her panty drawer and some spring will go out to hunt for purple flowers that wave above the rocks and grass in the April wind.

The pink penstemon is blooming in tandem with the globe mallow and the juxtaposition reminds me of a teenage girl headed for the beach, not quite blended.

I skinned a rabbit, dressed him out, removed his lungs and heart, connected, intact. The beating and breathing parts fit in the palm of my hand. I fed the lungs and heart, gift-wrapped in membrane, to the little red dog, and I am not sorry, not even a little bit, but he didn't even taste them.

There is a frog song serenade going on punctuated by splashes down at the creek. The miner's lettuce is making its brief show, but I haven't seen a mariposa lily yet. Sheridan Mountain anchors us all from the center of the ranch, no matter the season.

The smells make me pause. The brown and red and green all mixed together: alfalfa and dirt and manure and blood and wood fire that heats the irons and then burns the hair and the hide. Sweat and tired and horse piss.

We didn't brand the four smallest calves today. They lay in the corner of the pen napping. They are formed of clay, all boneless and soft, sleeping while their mouths move in sucking motions since warm milk is the only experience they have to dream about yet. They don't know to look ahead 'til the day they are stronger and bigger and must be branded, hard-fighting fish on the ends of our strings.

Poe wrote about the raven for a reason, and today I saw a pair of them, identical and sunblack. The female had a bundle of sticks in her mouth while the male swooped behind in a cover pattern as he followed her back to their almost nest.

I lead Gail's horse home through the creek while he drives the truck around, and the sun is making angles and shadows and dances on the west sides of the treetops. Instead of letting my mind wander, I hold it in place, in hoof-fall, and it rests.

He is waiting for us at the gate. The dogs, liberated from their chains, are ecstatic and present. His smile asks forgiveness for transgressions, harsh words he remembers saying now that the smells no longer assault us but wait harbored in our hair and clothes and membranes. We were working, doing a hard job, a dangerous job, and he was keeping me safe with shouted instructions while we worked. The hazard of lovers who labor together.

Now the horses swish their noses in the water, stirring up the goldfish that nap on the bottom of the trough. The jet streams are the only marks that give our days a place in calendar and time. Maybe the make and models of the vehicles parked about. We do an antiquated job, trapped in the amber of a world needing food. We deliver a protein source, harvested from the forest, nurtured by what grows up out of the ground without any help from us.

The shifts are changing, swallows retiring and making room for bats in the sky just as tea and water glasses make room for highball glasses, whisky on the rocks.

And so, we dance like the evening sun around the kitchen, smelling strongly of the work we do, while the transgressions burn away in Venus's and Jupiter's shine.

Witches and We

e were here. We knapped flint into exquisite points, mostly lost or broken now. We knelt, three abreast, at granite basins, grinding seeds and grains as the children played. Our men waited patiently for elk and deer at noondark springs while our women formed clay into pots. We gave birth, moved our homes to fresher water, made love, went to war, rolled heavy stones, grazed herds of animals on the slopes. Our old men smoked at sundown, looking over the rim of the canyon. We lived here. We died here.

On the Forest Service map, I can draw a line down the country from one seasonal or constant water source to the next. Seep springs. One is labeled Bill Murphy Spring, but I call it Earth Mother Spring after the day we found that cow with all those yearlings following her. Willow Springs. Brockmonte. Bull Water. And drop on down from there into that canyon where we followed those bear tracks to the place with those brighter green trees. There is usually a little hole of water there. Gail tells me it is called Granite Spring.

All along the route it is hard to take a step without walking on sherds of pots. Potsherds. Pieces of clay formed, smoothed, baked, painted, used. Broken.

I hike to the top of the ridge where I remember pottery scattered like potato chips after a child's birthday party. I noted this location several weeks ago as I rode. The cows I followed were moving too fast, anxious for water, and I had to keep on going, keep on doing the work. When I find the site again, it is with awe. Circle after circle of stones mark houses along the ridge. Pieces of kitchens bubble up from the churning *malpaís* earth. The dogs pant in the shade while I examine the remnant of who was here. I am walking through a village.

I carry home only what I think they'd have wanted me to have: a grinding stone made of pink granite, the one she treasured. She cried when she had to leave it behind.

It's like a dream, you know, riding along through the mouth of a canyon where there was a whole camp, a community. I have been here only a few weeks. Suddenly Gail reins to a stop in front of me and steps off. He leans down to pick up the perfect white bird point from the sand, loosed from a young boy's bow, a young boy banished from the women's circle for causing trouble or eating from the pot, but too young to go with the men on their hunt. Like a dream, Gail grins up at me and hands me the flint, makes a grand speech about giving his finds to the prettiest girl around. About six steps further on, the dream takes a turn when he asks for it back, his face serious. He says something about me seeing the real him, about truth in advertising as he slips the fragile bird point into his mouth and closes his eyes, thinking about who made it, who lost it, who trod this ground before us.

Letting what they made lie on his tongue. Honoring them.

I am reminded of Buck Ramsey's words: *Forgot we are what we do, and not the stuff we lay claim to.*

It's like a dream, you know, slipping that arrowhead into my pocket, swallowing hard, looking down the canyon at the past, but also at my future. It's like a dream, and I am living it.

I am an old man, smoking, with my back to the women's cook fires. Little boys with their arms full of wood run past, laughing, deaf to *hurry, hurry*.

What do they know of storms?

My daughter's daughter smiles shyly as she passes by, her belly swollen with summer's hot nights. Most of the village have already put their heavy cloaks at the bottoms of their sleeping mats, but I pull mine close about my shoulders. I know how Old Woman Winter must make one more joke before going to sleep.

I am an old man, smoking, facing the coming storm.

A new layer of snow fell in the night, covering the tracks we made yesterday. The ancient ones flew in on my dreams, from around the world, wearing their different feathers and fronds, to sit around my dream fire and ask their puzzled questions.

"Why are your people so scared of death that they give away bottles of their blood and swallow little pills and allow the wise men to put them to sleep and invade their bellies and shoot them with poison instead of allowing them to return to the sky and the earth at the right time? Don't they know that more people will always come?"

"And why do your children cough and forget to breathe and die from the bugs in the water and the food instead of growing big and strong and drinking from the rivers, letting the spirits live in their stomachs?"

"And why do your people move so fast, and yet become so fat as if all of the winters are going to be hard? Why do they flee from the weather as from an enemy, as if the snowflakes and raindrops and sun rays were arrows and stones?"

The ancient ones are gone in the daylight, but I go out to hike in the snow.

The *chindi* only cries at night.

The Navajo believe that when a person dies, a *chindi* leaves the body with the last breath. The *chindi* is to be feared. It is everything bad and unresolved in a person, left behind to infect others. The *chindi* is a witch.

I lie awake at Willow Springs and listen to the *chindi* cry. I am not afraid. Sometimes we need a witch or two. The Navajo cowboy told me that he has heard the *chindi* at headquarters, too, but only at night.

I don't know how to tell about poetry, about a snake in three parts, head buried in a shallow hole, rattles with ragged bloody flesh resting on the windowsill, long meaty body thrown onto the rock in front of the cabin. It went missing in the night. He came with aggression as I unloaded supplies on the cabin's porch. I wish shovels had longer handles, and how I hate killing, and how I needed some good karma after the carnage.

The next morning as I squatted out in the bushes with that same shovel, I heard something circling. I heard that something on my left, behind me, again on my right, and then in front of me. Not able to see until I could see, a little gray fox, head tilted to the side as if to say, "You see the darnedest things out here!"

We glimpse him often now for he has discovered that we put our food scraps and bacon grease atop the rock, the same rock where the body of the snake went missing. Surely the fox was the reason for that disappearance, a bonus feast unlooked for and not to be repeated.

So with karma comes poetry, the little gray fox, longer and leaner than he is tall, slipping through the oakbrush with no sound and leaving barely a track.

The snakes are crawling, looking to den up, and the cows are meeting us on the trails. They know it is time to make a move. The pear is abundant, and I see piles of scat loaded with seeds and smears of red.

I am bombarded with poems, tormented by poems, and sometimes there are five a day.

Twice now I've ridden alone along this canyon, trailing up remnant. The first time I went, I was riding Luna, an old mare who knows more about working cows than I ever will. On that day, I made mistakes. When I found a small group of cows going along the trail, I confidently turned them toward the hold-up, away from the seep spring where they were headed. Over and over, I fought them back onto *my* path, *my* way of doing things, the old mare obedient but mocking, as if she knew better. Finally, defeated, I allowed them to turn and go to water. Disgusted, I stepped off my horse in the dark shade of Bull Water, stepped off only to see an ancient spear point, almost perfect, lying in the dirt beside my boot. As the cows drank and I waited, four more pairs came out of the sunlight and into the gloom. I had split the bunch, the family, the social group, the tribe. We still made it to the hold-up on time.

The second time I went, I trusted my instincts and what I've learned, trailed up the little group napping in the shade on Cedar Mesa, took them handily to the horse pasture at Willow Springs; I drank a beer on the porch.

Last night I fed spaghetti to an old Navajo with red ribbons braided into his hair.

He sang, probably to ward off witches, when I showed him the spear point I found at Bull Water. Later I wished I knew that same song as he told of shooting an eight-year-old girl in Vietnam, one who had been selling cigarettes in camp every day until she came wearing something more explosive than a cigarette tray. His life pivots, you know, on that one day, that one bullet, that one child, and last night the firewater flowed. He told me I am guarded by the wolf and the chief, that arrowheads on the bottoms of my horse's hooves point always in the right direction. He sang the word for hummingbird and told me it is the same as the word for fighter jet.

I think he made up the part about the chief and the wolf, but I believe him about the hummingbird.

I spent fifteen minutes doing a search on Google and YouTube. The spooky guttural squawking sound that haunts some spring nights both here at headquarters and down at Willow Springs is a fox's mating call, like nothing heard before. The *chindi* mystery is solved.

But oh, I miss the witches.

KFC in the Dark

Ihave now been here on the Spider seven years and several months. Sometimes I get dull and think that perhaps our wonder years are behind us and we've reached the itchy years or the "What were you saying, dear?" years. When I first arrived, Gail said he was getting tired, worn down by riding through this country alone, but then I exclaimed over the vermilion flycatchers and the zone-tailed hawks and the hummingbirds feeding on the manzanita blooms. We've had tadpole and bear sightings and meteor showers and foxes and orioles and dragonfly moments and, just this spring, the nicest, smoothest, quietest cattle drive from Willow Springs to Cowboy Corral that anyone could ask for. And just this week we lay beside a pool in the remotest remote and I marveled at how beautiful our bodies were in the sun.

I don't think birthdays count as much as moments. Sixty is just a number. So is forty-six, but I'm designing a Tinkerbell tattoo. We are in the wonder years and we choose what duties, what obligations, will bring that wonder to an end.

The rocks and the bones and the feathers—the blood and the colors and the seasons—the songs of the creatures and the piles of scat and the flint chippings and the growth or scars of the fires . . . these all anchor us in place. They give us talismans to carry home, to show to our guests. "See? We dug that *metate* up out of the corral where we've penned hundreds of cows, and see? The *mano* was resting inside." But the most important things we carry home are the stories. We gather our stories and tell them in hopes of sounding a deep gong within another. To say, "We were here."

There is a rug from Turkmenistan on the floor of my office. I use it as a yoga mat. I wear wool slippers Gail bought in a market in Ashgabat. The Turkmen merchant insisted that one size fits all, and he was right. My favorite video footage in Gail's office is from Mongolia, where the people live with their animals and the women milk the mares and the houses are round. I am not that crazy about throat singing and I don't know if I should ever drink *airag*, but I would love to ride a little Mongolian horse. On the day he left Turkmenistan, airport security erased Gail's footage of Gurbanguly Berdimuhamedow's horse falling after the powerful president won the opening race at an enormous public event. Gail came home without the video evidence, without the image of Berdimuhamedow lying in the dirt, but he has the story.

A rawhide knife case rests on the shelf along with pottery from Hungary. The Hungarian herders gave us cunning utensils made from the horns of the Hungarian Gray Cattle. As we drove those herders and craftswomen to Elko, Nevada, up Highway 93, they kept indicating the terrain and saying *kecske kecske*. Goats. They left their spices and cloth bags of noodles with us.

Also on the shelf is a hat from Turkmenistan with camel hair lining and a wool hat from Afghanistan. Our friends from the south of France brought us wool scarves when they came to the ranch on their way from

Scottsdale to the National Finals Rodeo in Las Vegas. The shelf also holds an iron trident that Gail intends to make a handle for out of ash, not that we are going to tip any cattle over as they sometimes do in the Camargue. Propped up beside it is a wood-carved blab for weaning calves, given to him by his friend Jean-Luc who died of cancer. The little bag of bones is a game from Mongolia. The Mongolian rug is the hardest one to keep clean, but the rug from Afghanistan has the most beautiful colors. A bolo from Argentina hangs on the wall beside the stove. A rawhide rope from Brazil hangs on the hat rack. I dust the Seri carvings and caress their gentle curves.

I have never been to Mongolia or Argentina or Hungary or Afghanistan or Brazil or Turkmenistan. I've never eaten *moules* in the French Camargue. But I know the stories. I've heard the songs.

This ranch is painted over with story as well. When we ride in one part of Cottonwood Creek, Gail tells of Bill Murphy catching the wild ducklings and tucking them inside his coat and how they shit all over him before he got home to the dirt tank to turn them loose. I know the story of how Bill shot that cow when she ran off, again, into the side canyon coming up the trail to Willow. And, no, he was *not* shooting to turn her. I know the story of the time that the younger dogs treed a mountain lion and how Gail thought Salty was getting too old, barking at nothing over there in the wrong place, the wrong tree, only to find that he had treed two of her kittens down in the creek. Not so stupid in his old age. I think I'd like to name a dog Salty.

I like the story of Bill leading Mrs. Morris off that precipice and I can even point out the precipice. But I wasn't here.

Gail tells of the time a VW Beetle came by Willow Springs, headed to Sheridan Lake. The driver and his friend were going fishing. There are no fish in Sheridan Lake. There is no road to Sheridan Lake. There is no water in Sheridan Lake. But it is on the map. He tells of the time Ed landed a helicopter at Willow and took him for a ride. And the time he hobbled his horses on one side of the creek at Travis's Hole and settled in to sleep beside the fire he'd built. The horses started hopping home and he had to catch them in the middle of the waist-deep water. I know where Sleepy pulled Luna over backward on the trail when they were packing salt. And I know where Gail killed that bear and how nothing ate the carcass. It is a spooky story.

I know where he lost his father's Zuni watchband thirty years ago and I can't ride on that ridge without looking for it.

Some stories are told in tandem. Matt Bates and Gail tell the story of rolling up all of that old page wire and how they were going to pack it down to Alkaline Corral on Mack but he couldn't take the bouncing of those big rolls and bucked it off, scattered wire all over the flats. At the end of the story one of them always mentions that was the last time anyone drove a truck down to the North Benches.

Gail says, "But I've told you that story before." And it is true. He has. He has told me many stories about many places on this ranch . . . and I don't want him to stop. I want the stories—I crave the colors they paint onto this canvas for me. Stories in layers starting with the ancient ones and getting clearer up through time. And in the past several years we have gathered our own stories, like a shelf full of treasure.

Remember the time Linda ran under that tree limb? I patched your head and pulled cactus spines from your back and legs. And the time I came off of Luna in the creek? You didn't even slow down! Remember when I lost my slicker down in Tunnel Spring Canyon and we back-tracked to find it and how glad we were because it rained so hard while we were driving those cows to Horseshoe? Roscoe kept turning around, trying to put his butt into the storm. And then there was the time you led me off that trail-that-isn't-a-trail and I wasn't cinched up tight enough and my saddle slid up on Luna's neck? A cairn does not a trail make, Steiger.

And remember the night we cooked those elk steaks in the howling wind and then climbed in the tent and they were the best things we'd ever eaten? Well, maybe not better than the *moules* you ate in France. Remember the day I was up on Cedar Mesa and I could see you gathering cattle down below at Alkaline Tank and how I saw when you accidentally left those cows behind? It was like watching a silent movie. You went back and found them. Remember when those hunters sneaked over the dam all camo-ed up and how they crept into their blind and there we were . . . sitting in our chairs with whisky in our tin cups having fed cows and honked the horn and set up camp. Do you think they ever saw us? I am sure the deer did.

Do you remember that time down in Weber Canyon when you were holding my horse so I could crawl into that thicket to rock that cow out and the thicket was so dense I couldn't get a rock through the branches and you were yelling at me? We were brand new and I didn't know you very well. Now I would throw a rock at *you*.

And there was that time we saw that big cinnamon bear crossing Cottonwood Creek right by the trail crew's camp. And the time the oak tree fell on the corrals and we had that *Western Horseman* reporter with us. And the time I stepped off my horse at Jenkins to pick up that white arrowhead and you thought a bee had stung my horse. When you realized why I dismounted so fast, you said, "How good is it?" It is perfect. And the fall we shipped all those yearlings out of Cowboy Corral and it was an eight-hour round-trip to the sale barn? I stayed behind to tend horses and camp. You drove back in so late with a bucket of Kentucky Fried Chicken. We ate it in the dark, at almost midnight, passing the mashed potatoes back and forth. There was the time I found that big, round bottom of a clay pot sticking up from the trail and we covered it with dirt and came back later to dig it up. And remember that yellow cow you were so mad at and how we shipped her and Harry's son bought her at the sale barn? And the time those baby calves swam the bottom of Smith Canyon better than the grown cows did? When we showed the photos of that cattle drive to the Hungarian herders, they said, "Those babies can swim better than the moms," and you were saying the same thing at the same time and the translator and I both got chills.

I will be here for a long time to come, gathering more stories onto our shelves. Watch for rocks.

Crazy Love

Over a beer at one of the events that cluttered our calendar, my friend Matt gave me some advice. He said, "That new pack Gail bought you for your birthday? Load it. Load it with everything you need and lean it in the corner of your office. Keep it ready so that when the opportunity presents itself, you can shoulder it and go."

I wasn't born into a family that did things for recreation. We didn't go on many vacations or visit national or state parks very often. Plus, I grew up in Texas where, for the most part, land is privately owned. The state of that union is fenced with barbed wire, "No Trespassing" signs hung on the gates. The first time I helped Gail move cows from Willow Springs to Cowboy Corral, he said, "I'm going to work the ridges on either side of the trail as we go. If the motorcycles come through, just try to get the cows back on the trail best you can." I spent all day wondering why he allowed motorcycles on the ranch. The idea of public access and the recreational use of land was still new to me.

When I took my daughter on our epic seven-week camping trip in 2006, I read the printed material about day hikes but ignored the back-country information. In the Gila Wilderness, we hiked seven miles to Jordan Hot Springs and seven miles back out in one day, leaving only one hour, in midday, to enjoy the warm water. My justification was that we didn't have the gear. Behind that justification was the truth that I simply didn't have the knowledge to keep us both safe. Or the money to invest in packs and permits. I embraced the national parks in the atlas, risked car camping in a couple of state parks along the way, but I had no idea that the Forest Service lands were open to public use. Or grazing. Sometimes we wake up slowly.

The canyon begins with petroglyphs, a language we no longer know. She begins with mystery and falls away from there.

Perhaps those images, etched into the stones, are actually warning us away, describing her brutality rather than her beauty. She's all promises early on, seductive intervals, wide with trees and welcome.

But soon she turns her back on this invasion. She is changeable.

Just when I've baked in her furnace of rocks, white hot, she says, "Shade? Water? Why didn't you say so?"

She makes me wonder why I left the comfort of my clean office—fan whirring—my treasures around me as if the whole room were an altar, social media and information at my fingertips. This canyon would serve me up as a sacrifice, not even a satisfactory meal, to the creatures that inhabit her creases.

I am crazy to be here.

This canyon protects her moisture as the year ages, walls it up with stone above and below, makes a lover wonder if he'll ever get any again.

This morning I stand on an inflatable sleeping pad on a sandy river bank under a cottonwood tree and flow (well, almost) into a series of yoga poses, simple poses, while gazing at a muddy river at high water, receding day by day, on the Colorado Plateau of Utah. I am not rich. In fact, my income as filed with the IRS puts me below poverty level, and I have yet to afford health insurance even under the Affordable Care Act.

But, I am healthy. This morning I ate two sausages, blueberries, and granola. As I move awkwardly from child's pose up into a sun salutation, I lengthen my spine and feel it strive to be longer so I might touch the sky. I haven't had high fructose corn syrup in six months. Someday I will be able to do tree pose without falling over or thinking so hard. This morning I skip it.

Yesterday I saw a fox in the developed campground where the river runners spend the night before rigging their boats and pushing off into the water. He sniffed every fire ring and left only after I looked right at him. The tattoo on the inside of my wrist is healing slowly, a watercolor fox curled up in the night.

Paddling a rubber duckie in high water on the San Juan River is fun, but the pull-ins are hard and there is no going back if you completely miss one, which makes the whole endeavor scary. I move into Warrior I just as a Canadian goose family comes out of the bushes on the opposite shore: mom, dad, four chicks almost grown. I hope those goslings make all of their pull-ins today.

My coffee is cooling on the log beside me so I step out of Warrior II to pick it up and gaze at the swift water. I don't even know what time zone I am in.

I don't remember which meal I prepared that night, and it doesn't matter because I like them all okay and I don't get very hungry when I am as physically active as I had been since before 7:00 a.m. The hike was hard and the heat was brutal and it seemed all kinds of wrong, almost sinful, to build even the tiniest fire in the depression I dug in the sand . . . mesquite and sycamore sticks carefully arranged. My midday meal had consisted of naan spread with soft cheese and a pack of tuna, garnished with sun dried tomatoes. And water. And the barest shade while I sat on a boulder and let my feet air out, socks draped across my shoes.

Truth was, at the end of the day I could probably have eaten some jerky and been satisfied, laid down on my pad and slept all night without a meal.

But later I was glad I had gone to the trouble of cooking because they all showed up . . . all of them . . . and even though it was a crowd, there was enough. Like the loaves and fishes.

My family of birth showed up, in various levels of dismay, expressing concern about a solo hike in the desert in late May. I don't know if they have ever embarked on anything similar. They don't know the call that is in these rocks and these slots and these skies and these pools of water down low in the canyons. Some friends came, but I barred those that would echo the critics already present and allowed only the voices that begged me to take good notes and write it all down and don't leave out one single thing as well as those who begged to come along next time.

The lizard came and the hummingbird hovered above my colors, as did the jay and the hawk and the goldfinch and the buzzard, so high that he didn't know it was a meal. The fox had been there the night before, and the bear that morning, and the no-see-ums came en masse to talk smack with the ants about them both. The minnows waited patiently for their turn to feast when I washed my plate. The green sunfish showed me her spawning colors while resting gently in the circle of rocks prepared by her mate. I've come far enough to wish that, months ago, I had toed her sister back into the water after the expert left her to gasp and die. Toward the end of the meal the coyote sang a long, slow ballad and the mosquitoes added a whine and the wind gently blew them back to the creek while the bats moved in for dessert and the water picked up its pace, no longer slowed by the sun's heat. The moon rose in the pale sky above the canyon wall, a silent witness.

The map came to dinner and I marked my progress with a purple pen and left sentences in the journal that were inadequate to explain the level of my fatigue or triumph or disbelief or even the dinner party I had just hosted. The doubts came and the loneliness that isn't loneliness and the fear that I might miss something incredible and perfect. Dread of this hike being over came, too, until I played it Lao Tzu on the orchestra of my mind.

The stars offered a *digestif* that left me tipsy and sated.

Silence is relative. We know the cessation of certain sounds like motors or the neighbor's barking dog or the ringing silence after a powerful song when the music still courses through our memory and echoes in the air. Nothing is as silent as an unanswered *I love you*.

The wilderness is never quiet, and silence there is impossible. So many things singing and rustling and hunting and swooping and making conversation or home, running and trickling and dividing cells in noisy confusions. The human voice is out of place and the inescapable jet airplane sounds rude almost immediately upon my entrance into this place of no appliance hum/clock tick/television chatter. This entry was accompanied by the sound of my own feet falling on the trail and then the rock of the deep canyons and the brush of my pack against trees and bushes along the trail. When day was over I reclined in the sand, snugged into my bag, and listened as night tuned up, louder and louder as the darkness became full, an orchestra of life and earthspin.

Solitude is not relative. Yes, we can be alone in a crowd but to be truly alone, totally alone, inescapably alone, is a rare state. Yes, you can retreat into your private room and shut the door but the phone will ring or the e-mail plink will sound or your boss will wonder where you are tomorrow. 9-1-1 is almost always available, or the hotline where people talk carefully to the lonely and despairing. We are tied into this life of others by strong or tenuous threads of contact. Most of our lives are spent with someone in some way or another.

I left my home at 10:21 a.m. on Sunday, May 24. I saw another human again at 12:39 p.m., Wednesday, May 27.

Most people hike on trails. Most people don't turn off the cold water at the end of their shower to get one burst of scalding hot, an instant of intense heat.

Most people don't carry thirty-eight-pound packs, or love to sleep on sandbars, or get pulled into a four-day, three-night solo journey in the bottoms of canyons just to go where the water goes.

I found a purple feather and named it after you.

My brain kept up with the details: maps, log of how long from point to point (write it down in ink in a small notebook in my pocket), the battery level on my phone (for camera, not conversation), species seen and identified, landmarks noted, and after certain points start looking for a good place to sleep. My mind cataloged the meals I had left, how many sandwich bags of dog food remained in my pack, and how many SPOT points I should send to my support team and where. I am good at logistics.

My body is tough. My body is strong. My body is the reason I overrode the logic and fought for this hike. The baby toe on my right foot started hurting on the second day, but it will heal. I scrambled up and over too many boulders and barriers to count. I lowered my pack as far as my arm could go and then dropped it so I could turn and face the rock. Face to face with the rock. Find each foothold, each handhold, breathe deep and do not think of the hours and hours I will lie here until someone finds me if I fall. I swam a long deep pool, naked, floating my sleeping pad and my pack in front of me, my dog crying from the shore. He swam, finally. He could not endure being without me. My shoulders rebelled every time I lifted the pack. My breathing labored as I climbed. My shirt and camisole and bra were soaking wet. I kept going even when I wanted to quit. I pushed too hard. I slept like the dead, even in that wild.

I cried when I lost my map. I knew where I was, knew how to climb out to a trail I've ridden horseback dozens of times, but I cried. I wanted that map. I started laughing for joy when I saw the Gila monster, swimming just as I had, when I saw the king snake, a glorious stripe of color, when my little dog asked permission to come over and lie beside me in camp. I went from despair to *damn, I am a bad ass!* as the sun sank and I knew, really knew, what I had done on the second day. I loved where I was and I loved what I was seeing, and I loved me for being pulled here, for demanding that I go.

I saw that it was good.

I boiled one more pan of water and had Good Earth tea with gingersnaps and a small square of chocolate while the sky darkened and the tree frogs began to sing.

I sent a prayer heavenward for you with the black hawk.

I am the bear. I am the sycamore. I am the caterpillar being murdered by the ants. I am the Wilson's warbler perching high and catching the evening light. I am the chipmunk exploring camp. I am the minnow that will be labeled invasive, a species washed downstream and out of place.

I followed a fresh bear track all day on day four. I wanted to meet him.

Any sound from my throat sounded like thunder. My thoughts went from a roar to a trickle as I turned up that last long hard boulder slide that took me out of this canyon's mouth.

Reentry into human noise and human contact was startling. The excess of conversation after discovering that it is comfortable to say nothing. The sheer volume of food choices waiting. The complication of a house built and plumbed and finished and electrified after peeing in the sand and building tiny fires that smoked and crackled and talked back. But nothing was more startling than mirrors.

Why do we have them?

If the whole world is a mirror, then there is no clearer reflection than the self we see when we are alone in a wild place. I cannot rail in fury at the canyon for being so long, for being so rough, for being so hard, for I chose this route and she is but a seam in the crust, a place for succulence, columbine, monkeyflowers, clover, and creatures that wash their food in the night. She is a result of water and rock, and I am here to experience her. If I challenge her, I bang my shins on her boulders and leave my skin on their backsides. If I fight the bushes and trees I sit frustrated, caught in their indifferent embrace. If I approach her with joy and anticipation, a songbird perches above me and sings me through the day, sends gifts in the dusk.

While I am in this canyon, I am going forward. While I am in this canyon, I am wild woman with glorious hair and glowing skin and strength and a constant thirst that I slake with her waters, swallowing her minute insects and algae and amoebas, standing in awe of the springs that seep from the desert into her veins.

When I am home again, the mirror shows none of this. The mirror shows fatigue and scratches, a woman who is simple and plain with vanilla unremarkedness, tangled hair, and wrinkles around her eyes. The past envelopes me in its sameness. After all, I was only gone four days.

I rest. I mourn. I even howl on the inside. I try to tell it all, but there is no way.

In the dawn I sneak back to the mirror to find her.
And I do. The fire is in her eyes.

I returned home, not the same. And the house where I live was a mess. His son and friends had been here and meals had been prepared and the laundry piled up. And I told my story, but only some, thunder from my mouth that shut me up. And the chairs were out from around the table and I found a coffee cup in one of my plants. And the cheese was sweating, hard around the edges from being on the cutting board for too long. My pack, no longer thirty-eight pounds, shed bits of forest and creek bed and a small sack of garbage and leftover food, but it kept my secrets.

And so, I prepared two meals and we made love and I answered e-mails and I made phone calls and I studied those notes in that small notebook until I put it away. And I almost . . . just almost . . . forgot.

The next day I cooked for men, helped them find all the details they needed, and I watched them drive away to do a job. And the domesticated woman of me, the woman who is wife, mother, grandmother, sprinkled rosemary essential oil on a rag and started dusting and sweeping and . . . oh.

Scrubbing a bathroom. And oh.

The wildish part of me stopped doing. Started keening for what we were and what we are and all that we did in four days and every longing that led up to that first simple step. Those hardwonderful four days. Those brutalprecious four days. Those really fucking difficult climbs and scrambles and the getting lost. Those days of solitude and silence and wild and truth.

That night I ended up with plastic wrap around my left foot to protect the brand-new wound. There is black ink embedded forever in my skin. I walked up that canyon with a bear. Now he walks with me forever.

Night Notes

~Day is done, but the rocks in this canyon are still giving off heat.

~Soon I will rise from this nest I have made inside the hollow of my backpack and go over to the pool to watch the bats come to drink. My favorite show is about to begin.

~An oriole has come to visit, and me with no grape jelly.

~I just discovered a small zippered pocket inside my new sleeping bag. What words will I put in it for my future self to discover?

~Pieces of life lie about like clutter: tin cup, journal, headlamp, knife. What more do I need?

~I am my mother's only pagan child. Sleeping here, in this place, is less about nurture and more about being grown in a womb.

~Few things make me as happy as a campfire or a kiss.

In the End, It's All Details

Bid them all adieu
And give the merry shout,—
"The cowboy has left the country
And his camp fire has gone out."
~Ben Arnold

The West. A place where we've forgotten the campfires and the dirt and the work. We've made instead poems and music and reenactment scenarios, made it not so much about raising food as paying entry fees and cooking barbeque.

Icons only work if there is something of substance to back them up. The cowboy as icon only works if we keep the bedrock, the substance behind him. He is not some model of character or ethics or integrity, but a husband of the land, a grower of food. He is not an actor getting his share of the corporate take by reciting the words of scriptwriters and asking his horse to rear in time to the music. The cowboy is not a nostalgic touchstone from Saturday matinees, but a present-day reality, saddling his horse and getting greasy in the shop and building a fence. Six-guns and wooly chaps and parades and rodeos aside, the cowboy is a steward of precious resources, a caretaker of animals.

What would happen if I were to lay aside my boots and roots, move to The City or somewhere on the Chesapeake Bay? I would stand barefoot and bareheaded and watch the waves, avoid the jellyfish. Hope to see a whale. Not so very different from standing in leather and denim watching the clouds build hopeful, looking for dung and tracks in the dirt, avoiding the cholla and the snake. Hoping to see a bear cross the creek. Only the details would change.

Fall works is almost over and we rode in to Willow Springs to find the last few head. It is possible that we won't make them hike all the way out, sixteen miles, but will leave them down in the lower country where monsoon season was kind this year. Our main concern now is the tally. Where are the last thirty head? This is big country.

Gail steps off his horse to pick up a bird's nest from the ground. That first little autumn storm must have knocked it out of the tree. As we ride, we talk of the five cows we know are up on Smith Mesa, the tracks of two pair we saw down in the creek below Anderson Field, the old bitch he wanted to ship who is watering off in our little grand canyon—she won't show her face at headquarters and some warm winter Saturday we'll trail her up. The local sale is on Tuesdays.

We predict we'll find seven or eight off in Weber Canyon when we fight our way up through there one day this week. That place could use a good fire. We saw some tracks in Cottonwood. They must have gone around the fence where it burned several years ago. We'll kick them onto the mesa and hope to pick them up with the rest on our way through. Our tally is looking better. It improves again when we go through the gate up at Saddle Tank and hit a few more fresh tracks. We are riding against the tide, but at least the cows are moving in the right direction.

We talk of the last little branding we'll have before this works is over. Of the soggy bull calf in the group who is an early bloomer. He already acts and sounds like a grown-up bull. He is going to think us rude when we turn him into a steer. Plus, we've got to lay that one old cow down, the one we picked up two weeks ago. She has a horn growing into the side of her head, and we have to saw it off so she can birth the baby growing in her belly. She might not appreciate it, but we discuss how to let her step over the rope, how to lay her down gently.

We ride on. I wish we could explain to her that we are only helping.

We top out on the salt ground below camp. The ground is quiet here. A few weeks ago there were cow tracks everywhere, and we reined up often to scan the slopes and the ridges, to exclaim at the bunch on that hillside and the group up there working their way along the top and are those cows I see on the South Benches? Now last week's horse tracks are the most recent marks in the dirt. We are getting close. We've about done our job.

It takes almost four hours of steady riding to get from our headquarters home to our Willow Springs home. The finch's nest rides in the fork of my saddle. I am careful not to crush it.

We are in the lower horse pasture when we see Scout, a little paint horse getting on up there in years. He lives down here most of the time because of his ill temper toward the rest of the remuda. He's what cowboys call a cannibal or an alligator, and he always bites another horse right where the saddle goes. But, he's tough and athletic and willing. He's done his share of the work this fall. He's one of the team—and this evening he is in the wrong place. He and Linda should be in the upper horse pasture, not the lower. Linda's name is actually the Spanish word for pretty— pronounced *leenda*. We left her down here with Scout because she was sore-footed and needed some days to heal. She's the most willing horse I have ever ridden. We are having a love affair.

Gail whistles at Scout, wonders aloud about Linda, and then we see her up above in the rock pile. She nickers to her friends and starts our way, but stops abruptly and we hear a rock roll. We can't see the problem and ride on to camp wondering why the horses aren't following. In the lower water lot, the wire gate is completely destroyed. Some things will remain always a mystery.

I am in the cabin, moving around, thinking of making dinner when Gail comes to get me.

"She's stuck."

"Who's stuck?"

"Linda. In the boulder pile." We take our handsaws, a halter, gloves, a nose bag of grain and a rock bar, hike out to where we saw her last. And yes, she is well and truly stuck. She was grazing high in the rocks, on a nob of land covered with not only prickly pear and yucca, but boulders and knee-high grama grass. When she saw us ride in, she got excited, and as she exited the knoll, somehow a huge boulder rolled to block her way, also knocking several big chunks of skin and hair off her front legs. She is bleeding from the scrapes and trapped in a circle of rock and dense cactus. We use the pry bar to make stair steps, and I show her several times how to walk over them. We put the halter on her and I go before, keeping the lead rope totally slack. Gail gets behind her, the mildest pressure. She walks out of her trap slowly, carefully, gracefully.

When we get to the barn, I hold a dusty bottle of Cut-Heal in my hands. I know it would burn, and the bloody patches on Linda's legs are not bad enough to get infected. The process would mainly make *me* feel better. I can't explain it to her, can't explain the burn, so I put the bottle back on the shelf with fifty years' accumulation of medicines, tools, and dirt.

Once all the chores are done, we rebuild the wire gate in the blue dusk. The gate stick and three of the stays are snapped. The hot autumn day is now a very cool autumn evening. I walk over to the spring.

Blood. I kneel. The water has two rings of red in it and I think they are blood. Who is bleeding? But no. It is red algae growing around two submerged piles of cow manure. I lie down flat to see better. Not algae either. Rather, masses of minute red worms—strings moving in the water. They've made a whole world, a whole universe, out of that cow pat island. I call Gail over and soon he's kneeling in the muddy evening, too.

These years have given us routine. I know that in the morning I will turn on the blue flame under the coffee at 5:30 a.m., cook bacon and read a book by headlamp. We're packing salt to Scott's Basin for those cows we left on the big tank down there. I know which peaks will light up orange-pink first, that a quail will begin the morning call to worship, as inelegant as she is, a clumsy nun. I put my new nest on the windowsill. It is number five down here, but I might need it in my office at headquarters, just to see me through the winter.

I still play in the mud. During this week I find myself sitting with a pack horse loaded with salt at Alkaline Tank, waiting for Gail to bring that old gray cow who is always off by herself. She finally showed up and now can walk ahead of us down the hill and spend the winter where it is warm. The sun is lulling me . . . and then I see a flash of red in the water. Creatures keep surfacing and then diving, surfacing then diving. I know without a doubt that this tank was dry all last summer. They can't be fish. Maybe they are salamanders. Though similar in color, they are much bigger than the tubifex playing janitor in the spring at Willow. When I dismount for a closer look, I see strange creatures that look like miniature horseshoe crabs . . . small creatures with hard shells, long split tails, and dozens of wriggling red feet underneath.

I know what horseshoe crabs look like because in July I went to the ocean. Actually, I went to the Chesapeake Bay. My friend Travis, a scientist, picked me up at the airport and we drove toward a writers' retreat on the beach where, though we were on the East Coast, the sun went down over the bay as we faced west. When we topped the rise in Norfolk, Virginia, headed toward the bridge leading to the tip of the peninsula, the details got lost. For me it was just Ocean.

Ocean. Ocean. Ocean. Sky. Ocean. Bridge, tunnel, bridge, tunnel. Ocean. Ocean. Boat. Ship? Ocean. Bird. Seagull? Ocean.

Even after we got to the big house called *Way Over Yonder* where we were to spend the week, writing and retreating, I was still overwhelmed. I hugged and greeted my friends and fellow writers, but the pull was there. I wanted to walk down to the beach, but what shoes to wear? Travis suggested I go barefoot. I didn't put my shoes back on for six days.

Ocean. Sand. Waves. Salt. Ocean. Sky.

That night I wrote an e-mail to Gail to tell him I had arrived safely. All I could say was, "Ocean." His reply was something along the lines of, "Those poor people. They are going to have to put up with you in a whole new environment all week long." And it is true. Those poor people.

Soon though, the details began to make themselves known. Sand became dunes and beach and trumpet vines, the kind people plant in their yards in the Southwest. Blooming trumpet vines. The waves became high tide, low tide, white caps, glassystill mirror. The sky became sunset and sunrise and storm and clouds and wind and wide. Four long ships anchored in the bay and fixed my attention. I began to see the gray sand crabs as they scuttled sideways and turned pink and gold in the dusk. I saw the line of debris left by high tide, and even the huge horseshoe crab shells that stank in the sun. I saw the etiquette of writing *jellyfish* in the sand when the moon jellies ghosted through the surf. I was on the beach at all hours, heard the soundtrack of waves behind me as I walked back toward the house. I discovered that sand invades . . . my feet, my hair, my shower, my bed . . . and I didn't care.

I wrote, that week, of how my father had once scoffed at my adolescent dream of becoming a marine biologist when I became entranced by the photographs of diatoms that winked like jewels from the pages of my seventh-grade science book. "Twinkie, you've never even seen the ocean before!"

Now, over half a continent away, in the desert, I see miniature horseshoe crabs with red bellies rising to the surface of the monsoon-filled dirt tank in midday.

Four hours later, the gray cow through the gate and the blocks of salt dropped off under juniper trees, I head back toward camp. Gail is going a different way. He will check a water gap while I lead the pack horse back to Willow. Divide and conquer. When I pass Alkaline Tank I step off my horse and wrap two of the strange hard-shelled creatures in a tissue. They are still alive when I dump them in a dish of water in the cabin after I unsaddle. All I can think of is *amplexus.* What are these weird creatures and how do they reproduce? I am sorry to say that it doesn't come full circle. The tadpole shrimp do not need an embrace of any kind for fertilization, don't need copulation, pseudo or otherwise. Most of them are hermaphrodites. Some populations do not contain any males at all. Their eggs, not themselves, can live dried in the soil for years. Their broad carapace conceals the head and bears a pair of compound eyes. The abdomen is long, appears to be segmented and bears numerous pairs of flattened legs, the last pair often secreting both male and female organs. The tadpole shrimp, or *triops* or *notostracans* or, in old comic book ads, Sea Monkeys, are omnivores living on the bottom of temporary pools and shallow lakes. The species has been on this planet for three hundred and fifty million years. They are dinosaurs. Maybe that is a pretty big circle after all.

The dialog of land and animals won't go away when this cow works is over, won't go away when I retreat indoors. It will continue. It has been going on since before anything or anyone began to measure time, and the spin brings moments around and back again. Creatures, an ever-changing cast, move up to catch the early morning rays of sun as the edge of light and warmth creeps toward them. Rock squirrels in the tops of low trees, hawks and turkey buzzards in the tops of tall ones. Cubs and kits roll out of sleepy dens onto granite playgrounds. And on our side of the planet day begins, moves toward the moment when it is fully day and even the plants seek respite from what gives them life. As the turn goes on, always on, mothers and hunters and seekers and the weary sit again in that which is mild, the going now, rather than the coming, and rest in the final rays. The wise consider that it is always midday, fullbright, somewhere. The wiser rest in what is, right where they are. And the wisest simply rest.

A few nights later my wool stocking hat is welcome as the fire burns bright and then low, bright and low, at intervals for the evening hours. We are camped at Horseshoe Tank for perhaps the last time this year. We are on our way to headquarters with the last bunch of cows.

The sounds of cattle bedding down or cleaning up stems of alfalfa are all around us, and the horses are larger shapes among them in the dusk. I step away from camp to squat in the bushes. Through the dense branches of oakbrush, I see the glow, the glow of our next-to-last campfire. For the year.

Tomorrow we go back to clocks and bank balances and telephones. I haven't cared much about those numbers for weeks now. The sun and the moon and the animals and the miles have dictated our schedule, have made up our agenda. My hair and skin have absorbed the smells of our work and the weather.

Tired horses and cows walk slowly, but there is a lot to think about. And nothing to think about. No problems to solve. No way to rush the slow plod of long-toed horses who have done their jobs, just as we have.

In the morning I'll kick dirt over the last remaining burn. Our last campfire. For the year.

We've got this cow works saucered and blowed.

Wise Roses

What will I write about when I am old and my teeth are mossy and my hair is silver like my father's? What will I write about when I finally know the meaning of black and red and white?

I dreamed last night of writing wise things, things so wise I was no longer welcome at McDonald's or JCPenny. Things so wise that the dolphins met me at the shore and the wild roses waved at me as I walked by—the dung beetles camped beside my tent. I woke knowing only one old man's name and the words in the dream were just gray on the page.

Perhaps when I am old, I will write about how jobs are not living and paintings are the same as songs, about how seeds hold secrets and lonely is never bad and how we must carry things home with us tucked into the pockets of our cheeks. We can say, "See? We did the digging and the seeking. There is life out there."

Perhaps when I am old, I will not write at all . . . only sit and rock and watch and others will come and sit and watch with me and wonder why I rock and leave with impatient questions unanswered.

I dip my brain into

the hot gigantic swirl

of everything—

Lift it back out—

let it cool.

Everything

runs through the creases and folds,

drips down

the back of my neck.

Acknowledgments

Two eggs over easy, sausage patty, toast with strawberry jelly, apple juice, coffee, and a banana. Sometimes he had oatmeal, but as of 6:21 a.m., December 19, 2016, he will no longer place his breakfast order. Not many women in their mid-forties are blessed with the opportunity to say goodbye to a grandparent. There was a time when we thought he would outlive us all. I was in Texas helping care for him after an illness when this manuscript made its way through the peer review process. I received reader comments as well as their very welcome recommendations for publication, a plink of e-mail into my phone, while listening to the home health nurse tell my sister, my mother, and myself how to best care for this dear ninety-four-year-old man. It was a time of great upheaval in his life, a time of moving away from the only home he'd ever known, a time of giving up his car keys and his independent days. The next morning, I sat with my laptop while he read the newspaper. He looked up to ask what I was doing. When I told him I was working on the book, he shook his head and went back to his reading. "Well, I can't help you." There was no way to explain to him how much he has helped me with these essays. To Billy L. Moody (1921–2016) I owe an enormous debt, one of blood and family and love and history.

So many other people have aided in the writing of this book. First and always I am grateful to Editor Dearest, Andy Wilkinson, for his patience and wise guidance. I can't believe he still answers my e-mails after these dozen years of working together. Recently, he ruined my ability to read fortune cookies without a foray into the absurd.

I owe so much to Lily Rose Auker, a tireless and enthusiastic reader of everything I write. I know her secrets and she knows mine, but the one I won't keep to myself is that she is a kick-ass writer herself.

My appreciation to all the magazine editors who accepted and even paid money for some of the essays included in this collection, especially Kathy Wise when she was with *Cowboys & Indians*. She's the only editor I've ever encountered whose remarks consisted of one simple word: Perfect.

My thanks to Shellie Derouen for the purple meditation cushion. Thanks to the cowboy poetry gatherings who have invited me to perform my weird stuff over the past several years . . . well, they invited me . . . not sure they knew how weird my stuff would be. To Cheryl Estill for being my biggest fan and the best gift giver I know. To Alan Weisman for telling me to include some gossip in this book. To Pam Hinderlighter for the butterflies. To Travis Smith, Matt Bates, John Chiantaretto, Marilyn Hale, Ben Shiew, Molly and Paul Swets, Ivan Brown, Brent Reason, Fred Newman, Michael Jewel, Kristine Shmenco, Mary Matli, the McCall family, and Al, wherever you are. I hope you wintered well in Yuma.

Most of all, to Gail Steiger, my true partner, my lover, and my best friend. I got pretty naked in this book, and in order to do so, you had to strip and dance alongside me. Thank you for being willing. These are our wonder years, and you have a beautiful body.